# THE NEW RULES

## OTHER BOOKS BY JOHN P. KOTTER:

*Corporate Culture and Performance (with James L. Heskett, 1992)*
*A Force for Change: How Leadership Differs from Management (1990)*
*The Leadership Factor (1988)*
*Power and Influence: Beyond Formal Authority (1985)*
*The General Managers (1982)*

# JOHN P. KOTTER

# THE NEW

# RULES

## HOW TO SUCCEED IN TODAY'S POST-CORPORATE WORLD

THE FREE PRESS

*New York  London  Toronto  Sydney  Tokyo  Singapore*

The Free Press
A Division of Simon & Schuster Inc.
1230 Avenue of the Americas, New York, N.Y. 10020

Printed in the United States of America

printing number
1  2  3  4  5  6  7  8  9  10


**Library of Congress Cataloging-in Publication Data**

Kotter, John P.
    The new rules: how to succeed in today's post-corporate world/
John P. Kotter.
       p.   cm.
    Includes bibliographical references.
    ISBN 0-02-917586-0
    1. Executive ability.   2. Career development.   3. Success in
business.   I. Title.
HD38.2.K678   1995
650.1—dc20                      94-36216
                                           CIP

# CONTENTS

# THE NEW RULES

# INTRODUCTION

SUCCESS AT WORK FOR MOST PEOPLE MEANS A JOB THAT IS ECONOMI-
cally and psychologically satisfying, that makes a contribution to
society, and that supports a healthy personal or family life. This
book is about how paths to success at work have been changing
over the past two decades, and why. The material is based largely
on the experiences of 115 Harvard MBAs from the Class of '74.
For two decades I have been following these people's careers,
their choices, actions, successes, and failures. Information on this
group is supplemented by six other projects, all conducted between 1975 and 1993, involving another eighty-five executives,
most of whom do not have MBA degrees.[1] In total, the twenty-year
journey has been fascinating, with major implications in many directions.

The story that has emerged relates to an important set of
changes occurring in the business world, to individuals who are
sometimes controversial, to career paths that will surprise many
people, and to a powerful set of economic forces lurking in the
background. Although no one would have predicted this twenty
years ago, the key factors that have been affecting the Class of '74
are driven largely by the globalization of markets and competition.
This shift in the economy is altering the nature of managerial
work, career paths, the structure and functioning of organizations,

1

wage levels, and much more. At the heart of the story reported here is how 115 individuals have experienced this change and how many of them are taking advantage of it.

---

The roots of this work go back to 1968. At that time I was a graduate student employed by Professor Edgar Schein at MIT's Sloan School of Management. Schein had been following the careers of a small group of his alumni,[2] and while helping him, I learned about the power of tracking studies—where people are watched over many years. My interest in this kind of work was reinforced in 1972 when I discovered the Grant study—a huge effort which followed Harvard college graduates over multiple decades.[3]

The original concept was very simple. Select a group of students, gather as much background information on them as possible, and then watch the way their careers and lives evolve over a decade or more. I realized that such a project would require considerable time and energy, but I vowed to keep it a manageable undertaking that would be much less ambitious than the Grant study. Although I had some ideas regarding what I might find, they certainly were not very precise. My hope was simply that over time I would learn something interesting about these people, their jobs, and their careers.

In retrospect, this idea sounds both naïve and arrogant. Decade-long studies are almost never funded, and if they are, the money does not go to unknown assistant professors. When financial backers said no, the project survived only because Dean Larry Fouraker at Harvard Business School said he would find the money somewhere. "Do it," said Fouraker. And I did.

With the cooperation of 115 Class of '74 MBAs, I collected yearly questionnaires starting in January 1975, conducted some interviews, and for half the group, gathered extensive psychological test data. On basic dimensions like age, gender, and socioeconomic status of parents, the 115 were similar to the overall class, so I am confident they are not an unusual group. Most were very responsive over the years; 90% sent back each questionnaire.[4]

A strategy of relying mostly on questionnaires has turned out to be both good and bad. This approach has not allowed me to get to know many of the 115 in any deep personal sense, but it has kept the project manageable in terms of time and money and has allowed me to follow over 100 people instead of just a dozen or two.

I have often wondered why these 115 individuals stuck with the study all these years. No doubt part of their loyalty was due to a very natural inclination to want to help a potentially good cause. But I also think that many of them found pausing once a year and thinking about what they were doing and how they felt about life to be a valuable experience. I certainly found it fascinating to watch and listen to this group of my contemporaries. Thinking about their experiences has helped me put my own life into a broader perspective and helped me think about the choices I have faced.

In the original plan, I was going to begin a book after ten years. When I tried to write about these people in 1983, I found that their stories were both incomplete and difficult to understand. Eventually, I stopped writing but continued collecting information. Over the next few years, I realized that other studies I had been conducting could provide useful insight into the Class of '74. Finally, around 1990, everything began to crystallize. By 1992, the total amount of information gathered from the 115 MBAs filled eight filing cabinet drawers. I sorted through all this in stages starting as early as 1979. The synthesis reported here was done in 1990, 1991, and 1992. This manuscript was written in 1992 and 1993.

At least five different books could have resulted from this single project. One is historical ("The Class of '74"). One is aloof and very analytical ("The New Economic Environment"). One is psychological and developmental ("Becoming an Executive"). There is also a social commentary ("Success?"), and one that focuses on careers and success at work. To a limited degree, this manuscript incorporates all five, but it clearly emphasizes the last (careers/success).

Readers may wonder how anyone can generalize from a study

of a relatively small group of Harvard MBAs to a much broader population. I have thought a great deal about this question and am personally convinced that many of the lessons one learns from the Class of '74 are relevant to a large group of people. These lessons are consistent with what I have found in six other studies conducted over the same time period but which involved a much more diverse group of individuals. Ultimately, readers will have to judge for themselves whether I am right or not in this regard.

The issue here is similar to watching sports stars. Even though generalizing from unusually talented individuals to other people is difficult to do well, nearly everyone can learn something valuable about basketball and football by watching very successful players. I think the same can be said about looking at a group of people who have been very successful in business.

On the pages that follow, I will be describing the experiences of 115 people as well as the conclusions I have drawn from watching them and others over the past twenty years. The most basic of these conclusions are summarized briefly in the exhibit on the next page. That exhibit also lists where in the book each item will be further discussed. For now, let me just stress four points:

1. What is required to succeed in business and in management has been shifting over the past decade or two in some very important ways. Career paths and approaches to work that were winners throughout much of this century are no longer paying off well. Nevertheless, significant numbers of people are still trying to use the old strategies, with frequent encouragement from most major institutions: big business, big labor, government, and education.

2. A shift in what is required to succeed is being driven by many factors, none of which is more important than the globalization of markets and competition. Globalization is increasing the rate of

## THE NEW RULES

### New Realities

Do not rely on convention; career paths that were winners for most of this century are often no longer providing much success (Chapter 2).

Keep your eyes on globalization and its consequences; everything is changing, offering both gigantic new opportunities and equally large hazards (Chapter 3).

### New Responses

Move toward the small and entrepreneurial and away from the big and bureaucratic; speed and flexibility are winning in an increasingly competitive world (Chapter 4).

Help big business from the oustide as well as on the inside; huge opportunities exist for consultants and other service providers (Chapter 5).

Do not just manage; now you must also lead to help make organizations winners (Chapter 6).

Wheel and deal if you can; huge opportunities exist in financial and other deal maker careers (Chapter 7).

### Underpinnings

Increase your competitive drive; high standards and a desire to win are essential today and in the future (Chapter 8).

Never stop trying to grow; lifelong learning is increasingly necessary for success (Chapter 9).

change and producing both more opportunities and more hazards. Put succinctly, people who are prospering nowadays are finding ways to capitalize on those opportunities. Those who are failing are being strangled by the hazards.

3. Most of those who are doing well today in business and management are capitalizing on globalization by pursuing career paths that are less linear, more dynamic, and more unstable than mid-20th century norms. They are also increasingly associated with small business and entrepreneurship, not the big and bureaucratic "corporate" world, with consulting and other services that help big business from the outside, with leadership, not just management, and with financial deal making.

4. Successful use of these new strategies requires high standards, a drive to compete, self-confidence in competitive situations, and a willingness to keep growing and learning new things. In the current economic environment, people who fear competition, want security, and demand stability are often sinking like rocks in water.

These conclusions and others have significant implications for how people should manage their careers today, for how both big and small corporations should be run, and for education at all levels. Before finishing, I will explore these issues with an eye toward our coming transition into the 21st century and with a particular interest in how we can help more people to succeed despite a difficult economic environment.

# PART I

## NEW REALITIES

# 1

---

# IS THE AMERICAN DREAM
# DEAD?

---

THEY GREW UP IN AN ERA OF GREAT EXPANSION IN THE UNITED
States, a time that gave renewed life to the concept of the American dream. Kevin Johnson was one of them.[1] Born near Chicago
on March 27, 1946, he was raised in an environment where upward mobility was the order of the day. In 1954, Kevin's father
was promoted from salesman to sales manager. The family moved
out of their older two bedroom home located just ten minutes from
Comiskey Park and into a four bedroom split-level in Winnetka
with a two car garage, a barbecue patio, and a real backyard. The
economy was a mighty engine back then. Gross national product
in the United States increased in real (1992) dollars from 213.4 billion in 1946 to over a trillion in 1968, the year that Kevin and a
group of early baby boomer peers graduated from Stanford. During this period, American businesses set the standard for the world
and were exceptionally successful. No less than 75 of the world's
100 largest revenue-producing industrial firms in 1955 were U.S.
based.[2]

America's global domination was already slipping when Kevin
completed college and went to work for Motorola, although few of

us noticed the downward trend. After four years of work in the electronics industry, Johnson found another wave that was still on the rise—the movement toward MBA education.* In September of 1972, he came to Boston and enrolled as a student at Harvard. Two years later he finished the program and, despite the recession, received four good job offers. When he started work in June of that year, he felt on top of the world.

Kevin's optimism was fed both by his own early history and by the business school experience. In Boston, he and his classmates were told many times and in many ways that some of them were destined to be very important people in the world of industry. This promise of professional success from an MBA education was even confirmed by a *Fortune* article that appeared as they were taking their last exams. Focusing on HBS graduates from 1949, the title of the piece was "The Class the Dollars Fell On." The subheading told readers that in twenty-five years, the "Class of 1949 has risen to power, prestige, and riches."[4] Those pictured in the article included Jim Burke, the then President of Johnson & Johnson, Sumner Feldberg, the Chairman of Zayre, Vincent Gregory, Jr., the President of Rohm & Haas, William Hanley, Jr., the President of Elizabeth Arden, Peter McColough, the Chairman of Xerox, M. G. O'Neil, the President of General Tire, and John Shad, the Vice Chairman of E. F. Hutton.

I doubt if any of us back then fully recognized that the economy was beginning to undergo a very fundamental change. After twenty-five to thirty-five years of growth and prosperity—the period in which the Class of '49 built their careers—the environment was suddenly becoming more global, more competitive, faster moving, more unstable, and a lot tougher. Real GNP increases slowed greatly. The net result was a huge decline in the acceleration of the living standard for the average U.S. citizen.

---

*In 1972, the year Kevin applied to business school, 32,677 people received MBA degrees compared to 2,314 the year after he was born.[3]

From 1947 to 1973, Americans became accustomed to an economic growth rate that would double their real standard of living every 1.6 generations. After 1973, the economy slowed to the point where it required twelve generations to achieve the same result.[5] For some people, living standards actually declined. A world in which people become twice as prosperous economically every generation or two is radically different from one in which there is little change from grandparents to grandchildren. (See Exhibit 1.1)

Most people, including Kevin, did not fully realize until the 1980s that something very fundamental had changed about the time of the first oil shock. Even today, all the reasons for and implications of this shift are not entirely obvious. But today we do know that the high expectations molded by the quarter century after World War II do not fit well in a new age of tough global competition.

It was in this new age that Kevin and millions in his generation began their careers. Pumped up by a quarter century of growth and good times, they were shot out of a cannon in the direction of a brick wall.

EXHIBIT 1.1

Median Family Real Income in the United States

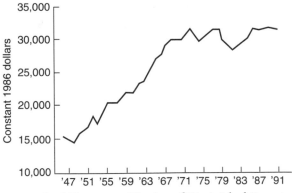

*Source:* Paul Krugman, *The Age of Diminished Expectations,* Cambridge, MA: MIT Press, 1994, Page 5.

By the early 1990s, more and more people who were Kevin's age and younger began to wonder if they would be able to live as well as their parents had.* Charlie Kolowski, a grade school buddy of Kevin's, was laid off from a middle management job in 1981, spent fourteen months unemployed, and then accepted with misgivings a job with less responsibility and income than he had had before. Brent Farmer, the tight end on Kevin's high school football team, saw his salary at a Chicago auto parts company drop by 15% in 1989. Elizabeth Bloom, the seventh grade love of Kevin's life, decided in 1985 to return to the workplace after her two children started school but only received offers for service jobs paying $5.00 to $6.00 an hour. All three, along with millions of others, began to seriously question the American Dream of ever increasing prosperity. In their study of people born in the United States between 1946 and 1964, Paul Leinberger and Bruce Tucker concluded pessimistically "that the 75 million members of the baby-boom generation . . . will likely be the first generation in American history that will not do better economically than its parents."[7]

Times were tough. Even Kevin found a business climate that was faster moving and more dynamic than anything he had been led to expect. An acknowledged film fanatic who today owns over 300 movies on videotape, Johnson had seriously considered trying to get a job in Hollywood both in 1968 and in 1974. But when he sought counsel, nearly everyone advised against such a move. "Again and again I was told that work in the motion picture industry would be too unstable and too risky. People told me to go to a company I could count on, like IBM." He reluctantly accepted this advice, began work in June 1974 as a financial analyst in the elec-

---

*At least one source has reported that in 1991 Americans aged thirty-five to forty-five were only half as wealthy, in real dollars, as their parents were at a comparable age.[6]

tronics division of a Fortunc 500 company, and received relatively predictable promotions in 1975 and 1977. Then, unexpectedly, his employer encountered new competition from the Far East and simply stopped growing. "The firm had been experiencing revenue increases of close to 10% per year, year after year. Then, suddenly, we had new competition, sales growth dropped to nearly zero, and we actually lost money. Opportunities for fast promotions disappeared. Even worse, some people lost their jobs. The whole experience was unsettling."

Five years later and at another firm, Kevin's future plans were once more disrupted when his division was sold, his mentor quit, and his fast track again disappeared. "I thought I had done thorough homework on the firm and the people involved before I accepted the job. And then suddenly, the business was sold and the division general manager (a strong supporter of mine) was replaced. The new owners reorganized everything and basically canceled the strategic program I was working on. It was déjà vu all over again. I'm sure my wife would say I was impossible to live with for about six months. I was very angry, anxious, discouraged, and uncertain about what to do next." Two weeks before Christmas in 1986, he quit the "stable" world of large industrial corporations and accepted a job elsewhere.

Compared to some of his Class of '74 colleagues, Kevin's setbacks have been minor. Over one-third report that they have been fired or laid off at least once. Bill Jameson was out of work, except for a few "consulting" assignments, for nearly two years. Bill says the stress during this period nearly ruined his marriage. Some have seen their entrepreneurial ventures fail in a difficult economic environment. Troy Gleason lost nearly half a million dollars when his startup went bankrupt. At one time or another, virtually all of these people, have been very discouraged, as reality did not keep up with their expectations. After getting into a fight with her boss, receiving virtually no pay raise, and being passed over for a promotion, Karen Glister wrote in a 1980 correspondence: "To think that I spent many thousands of dollars to get an MBA, put in sixty-five hour work weeks, and suffered some pretty bad bosses, all FOR THIS?"

Times were tough.

––––––––––

For twenty years now, I have been following Kevin and 114 of his MBA classmates. These have often been difficult years, character-ized by a tough economy, a crowded labor market created by an increasing abundance of baby boomers, and limited opportunities in firms that have stopped growing. Under these circumstances, how well have Kevin and his fellow MBAs fared?

They started work in June 1974. The single largest employer for the entire class was Citicorp. The bank hired twenty-one students, or about 2.6% of those graduating. Other major employers in-cluded Ford, Arthur Andersen, General Foods, Exxon, Goldman Sachs, W. R. Grace, Procter & Gamble, Baxter Laboratories, Boise Cascade, McKinsey, IBM, and Hewlett-Packard. With few excep-tions, their job titles were rather modest: assistant salesman, grain merchant, consultant, manager of business analysis, senior ac-countant, corporate planning specialist, project manager, research analyst, quality assurance engineer, senior estimator, sales repre-sentative, loan officer, master scheduler, financial analyst—plus many more. About 30% of these positions could be called market-ing or sales jobs, 17% were in finance, 13% were accounting or control oriented, 13% were in general management, and 10% were in production or operations. The majority of these positions were very similar in one important aspect—they did not require much supervision of others. Instead, the work was professional in na-ture, where individuals applied expertise learned in school in com-bination with special competencies that they were taught by their employers. They analyzed business data, bought or sold merchan-dise, audited accounts, scheduled production flows, designed sys-tems for managing cash, and gathered information for market re-search. Fewer than 5% held jobs in which they were responsible for more than a dozen other people.

On average, they stayed in those positions for eighteen months[*] and with their first employers for $3\frac{1}{2}$ years. Then between 1975 and 1992, the typical person in Kevin's class changed firms twice and held seven different jobs.[†] The journey was sometimes exciting and dynamic, but for most of them it was far from smooth or easy. Career problems were exacerbated by turbulence off-the-job. Some went through trauma trying to conceive children and failing. A few have lived with the sorrow of serious birth defects in their offspring. Health problems have led to the death (at age thirty-eight) of one class member and to numerous significant illnesses. More than one has had a spouse walk out on him, at least one has had his house burn down, and many have been caught in crazy lawsuits, in-law crises, and more.

But despite all the problems, most have progressed in their careers astonishingly well. Between 1975 and 1992, they moved out of their professional roles first into managerial jobs, then into either entrepreneurial situations or executive positions. In 1975, 7% of them could be classified as executives, entrepreneurs, or owners. By 1992, nearly 80% rated that classification. In 1975, 13% reported that general management was their primary functional focus. In 1992, over 50% described their jobs this way.[‡] The budgets they controlled grew from almost zero to millions of dollars per year. Subordinates also grew from almost none to, in some cases, hundreds or even thousands. Their job titles confirm this increasing power. By 1992, nearly 50% of the group were called chairman, vice chairman, president, managing director, CEO, COO, or owner. Another 30% were executive vice presidents, senior vice presidents, group vice presidents, vice presidents, general managers, or partners.

---

[*]Forty-four percent stayed for one year, 41% for two years, 9% for three years, and 6% for four or more years.

[†]For more detailed statistics on job changes, see Notes 8 and 9.

[‡]For more detailed statistics see Notes 10 and 11.

With this power has come growing affluence. The typical person's income increased more than tenfold between 1974 and 1992, going from $18,000 to $195,000. Net worth increased 100 times, to over a million dollars. That is nearly as much wealth as the combined net worth of two dozen families in the United States.* For the most successful half of the class, the numbers are much higher.† At the low end, only 2% of the group had total family income less than twice of what is typical in the United States.‡

Incredibly, this group has done even better financially than the fabled HBS Class of '49. In 1992 dollars, the class that rode post-World War II prosperity had incomes of about $150,000 at their 25th HBS reunion. The Class of '74 earned more before their 20th reunion. The 49ers had an average net worth of slightly over $700,000 (1992 dollars) twenty-five years after school.[14] Kevin and his colleagues have also exceeded that figure before their 20th reunion. (See Exhibit 1.2.)

If current trends continue, the typical person in the Class of '74 will retire with a net worth around eight million dollars.[15] The top 5% will have over $100 million. *In non-inflated currency, most will accumulate wealth over ten times as large as that held by their parents.*

In 1992, at age forty-six, Kevin made $255,000 as the Executive Vice President of a $150 million a year software firm that specialized in interactive video production. This was his third employer and his eighth job since graduation (see the profile on Page 18). He was married with two children and had a net worth of a little over $1 million. In late January 1993, he reported that he was generally quite satisfied with life. At times, he admitted, he wished he were president of his firm and owned more of its stock. But overall, he felt his job was interesting; "I finally made it into the video business!" And he expressed great enthusiasm for his family.

---

*Median net worth for all U.S. households in 1989 was $47,200. Median net worth for households with family heads aged 35–44 was $52,000 (1989)[12, 13]

†Median 1992 net worth for the top quartile of the class was $5,000,000.

‡Median net worth for the bottom quartile of the class was $275,000 in 1992.

EXHIBIT 1.2

Income and Net Worth History for 115 MBAs

|  | 1974 | 1978 | 1983 | 1988 | 1994 |
|---|---|---|---|---|---|
| Income* (median) | $18,000 | $ 37,000 | $ 84,500 | $ 142,500 | $ 260,000 |
| Income* (mean) | $18,500 | $ 48,000 | $131,000 | $ 264,000 | $ 410,000 |
| Net Worth (median) | $10,000 | $ 50,000 | $250,000 | $ 600,000 | $1,200,000 |
| Net Worth (mean) | $46,300 | $105,400 | $606,800 | $1,687,000 | $2,789,900 |

*Salary, bonus, and equity appreciation for entrepreneurs

These figures for the Class of 1974, based on a sample of about 14% of the overall group, are consistent with data based on questionnaires returned by 29% of the Class of 1973 at their 15th reunion. In 1988, the '73 group reported median income of $160,000 per year and median net worth of $900,000 per person. Some percentage of the net worth figure is due to inheritance, but for the typical class member, that figure is low, around 5%.

Not all of his classmates are as happy as Kevin. Some have had expectations that they have not been able to fulfill. But most like their work very much. In 1992, over 40% reported they were extraordinarily satisfied or very satisfied with their jobs; at the other extreme only 3.2% said they were very or extraordinarily dissatisfied. Ninety percent are married. Most have children and are very happy with their families.* Within this group, success on the job has rarely resulted in an unsatisfying personal life (see Exhibit

---

*Regarding satisfaction with their families in 1993:

| Extraordinarily Satisfied | 28.1% |
|---|---|
| Very Satisfied | 33.3% |
| Satisfied | 24.0% |
| Somewhat Satisfied | 5.2% |
| Dissatisfied | 10.4% |

# KEVIN JOHNSON

PROFESSIONAL

| 1987–1993 | Halio Graphics | Waltham, MA |

- Executive Vice President, in charge of Marketing, Sales, and Administration (1991–1993).
- Vice President of Marketing (1987–1991).

| 1980–1986 | Bartuk Systems, Software Division | Sunnydale, CA |

- Vice President of Marketing (1984–1986).
- Senior Product Manager (1981–1984).
- Product Manager (1980).

| 1974–1979 | Tallon Industries, Electronics Division | Newark, NJ |

- Marketing Manager (1977–1979).
- Senior Financial Analyst (1975–1977).
- Financial Analyst (1974).

| 1968–1972 | Motorola | Chicago, IL |

- Electrical Engineer and Systems Analyst.

EDUCATION

| 1972–1974 | Harvard Business School | Boston, MA |

Masters in Business Administration, second year honors. Member of Finance Club and writer for "The Harbus" student newspaper.

| 1964–1968 | Stanford University | Palo Alto, CA |

B.S. in Electrical Engineering, minor in Economics. Member of Student Senate, Academic Standing Committee, and junior varsity baseball team.

PERSONAL

Background: Born in 1946, raised near Chicago.

Marital Status: Married in 1978 to Debra Moreton (V.P. at a Boston bank). Two children, ages 10 and 8.

Interests: Motion pictures, sailing, running, travel.

Recent Reading: *Truman* by David G. McCullough and *The Firm* by John Grisham.

1.3). Overall, less than 12% reported in 1992 that they were dissatisfied with their overall lives.*

Hearsay knowledge of all this has been attracting hundreds of thousands of people each year to business programs. In an age of limits, the Dream seems to live on for some.

EXHIBIT 1.3

Work and Non-work Satisfaction in 1992
Among 115 Class of '74 MBAs

| | | No | Yes |
|---|---|---|---|
| Satisfied with work? | Yes | 1% | 80% |
| | No | 2% | 17% |
| | | No | Yes |

Satisfied with non-work
aspects of life?

*Source:* Based on answers to sixty questions asked between 1989 and 1991.

So why have they done so well?

A part of their economic success is attributable to smarts and the advantage of a degree from Harvard. But intelligence and educational privilege explain far less than one might expect. Large numbers of people at the Graduate School of Arts and Sciences at

---

*Their "overall satisfaction" with life was measured on a nine point scale going from extraordinarily dissatisfied to extraordinarily satisfied. Anyone reporting 1, 2, 3, or 4 constitutes a "dissatisfied" answer.

Harvard had better test scores in 1972 than these HBS students and yet are earning much less today. Even within this group of MBAs, those with higher incomes in 1993 did not score better on intelligence measures while in school than did their lower-earning classmates. To the contrary, those with higher incomes today appear to have scored slightly lower on the business school admission test (the GMAT).*

If the HBS degree and the connections it implies were key, the earnings spread between the top and the bottom of the class would not be huge. Yet it is. By the time they retire, the top 10% of the Class of '74 will probably have accumulated wealth that is one hundred times greater than the bottom 10%. One hundred times.

Their economic success is not well explained by the privilege of their family backgrounds either. Few grew up in rich circumstances. Many came from the upper middle class, but on average, they appear to have done considerably better in their careers than most of their peers with similar socioeconomic backgrounds. Within the class itself, parental wealth and education do little to explain income differences in 1993.†

The story of their success is both more complex and less conventional than "rich boy does well" (or "smart girl" or "well-connected child"). Indeed, conventional explanations are of limited use here because unconventionality itself is a key part of the story.

---

*See Exhibit 8.4.
†See Exhibit 8.3.

# 2

## UNCONVENTIONAL
## CAREER PATHS

JEREMY KING GREW UP IN A MIDDLE-CLASS FAMILY WITH NONE OF
the privileges associated with real affluence. He attended Alberson
College, a good but not outstanding university, worked for five
years, and then got an MBA. Two decades later, he is by any rea-
sonable measure an exceptionally successful person.

The youngest of four children, King was born near Toronto on
June 8, 1946. His father was employed in the same medium-sized
manufacturing company for which Jeremy's grandfather had also
worked. His grandfather was a highly skilled mechanic. Jeremy's
father began his career after eight years of schooling and over
three decades rose to become a plant manager.

From 1963 to 1967, Jeremy commuted to a university near his
hometown, graduating with a degree in economics. He then accepted a job in Canada with General Motors and worked there for
five years before coming to graduate school. During the summer of
1973, King worked for an investment management firm in Boston
and met the woman who, six years later, would become his wife.
At the end of his MBA program he accepted a position as a financial analyst in London for another large U.S. manufacturing company.

Between 1974 and 1979, King worked in three different jobs, in three different cities, finally relocating back in Canada (see profile on the next page). When asked in 1979 if he felt successful, he replied with a qualified yes. When asked to define success, he said: "Basically, this means being happy through having achieved one's goals both on and off the job."

In 1980, King launched a real estate venture with $10,000 of his own money and a few hundred thousand dollars of capital from other sources. The startup was not easy. Even today one can detect a distinct edge in Jeremy's voice when he describes those events. "I decided to try, on a small scale, a concept that had been used successfully in the United States but not yet seen in Canada. All that was required was a great deal of abject begging on my part. But eventually, we did succeed in putting together the deal." His wife managed this business, although he often spent twenty hours per week working on it himself. Laboring as a big company executive from 8:30 A.M. to 6:00 P.M., he then became a real estate entrepreneur from 8:00 P.M. to 11:30 P.M. When asked about his long hours back then, he recently said: "I really didn't have enough time for everything and I didn't like that. But working for myself was fun. I didn't have to wear a tie. The business strategy was mine and I had a lot of confidence it would work. Under those circumstances, the long hours didn't seem that burdensome."

In 1981, King switched employers, accepting a promotion into a senior-level planning position at yet another big manufacturing firm in Montreal. At age thirty-five, he was one of the youngest people in the company's top management. In an interview conducted shortly after joining this firm, Jeremy seemed genuinely excited about his new corporation. But when asked about the long term, he spoke hopefully about his real estate business.

Almost from the beginning, his personal venture was profitable. In the economic environment at that time, more and more businesses were interested in leasing instead of owning certain kinds of real estate. Jeremy offered them a high-quality leased product. Furthermore, it looked as if traditional real estate players in Mon-

# JEREMY KING

## BUSINESS EXPERIENCE

Foxworth Real Estate, Montreal, Canada (1980–1993)

- Managing Director and President (1985–1993)
- Founder and part-time executive (1980–1985)

Furgeson International, Montreal, Canada (1981–1985)

- Group Marketing Manager, International Group

Carnegie Chemicals, London, Brussels, Montreal (1974–1977)

- Director (1978–1980)
- Financial Analyst (1974–1977)

General Motors, Canada (1967–1973)

- Purchasing Agent

## EDUCATION

Harvard Business School. Received MBA, 1974.

Alberson College. Received B.S. in Economics, 1967.

## PERSONAL

Born near Toronto in 1946. Youngest of four children. Father a manager in a manufacturing enterprise. Mother not employed outside the home.

Married Susan Atkinson in 1979. Two children.

Quote: "During my two years in the MBA program, I learned a lot, although I don't remember many of the specifics. What I do remember is basic approaches to problems, opportunities, and business situations. (1983)"

treal had misjudged demand for this new product. In 1983, King expanded his business and took defensive measures to try to keep out competition. Cash flow was strong. With money from multiple sources, he and his wife bought a house, renovated part of it, and made plans for the arrival of a child.

In February 1984, Jeremy reported he loved being a father and he loved his real estate business. His enthusiasm for his primary job was lower. Given a list of twenty-two problems and asked which he had experienced in the 1974–1984 decade, he checked only three: coping with corporate politics; not having enough time for work, family, and self; and not having a mentor or role model. In his big-company job, he said he sometimes felt as if his talent and hard work were simply wasted. The contrast with his small business was often glaring.

In July 1984, with self-confidence and skills coming from experiences in three different companies, three different business functions, and three different countries, King quit the corporate world to work full time for himself. Although some of the expansion of his real estate ventures could be funded out of cash flow, he raised additional money so he could grow more quickly and leave fewer opportunities for competitors. In 1986, he also brought in a business school classmate as a partner to help run the enterprise. By 1987, they employed twenty people. In 1988, King took out a sizable loan and bought out most of his early partners. Taking a risk in doing so, he was convinced this move would pay handsomely long-term. So far, he has mostly won his bet despite a very difficult real estate market. Jeremy's customers seem to love what he has to offer.

Dealing with a difficult real estate market has been tough at times. Dealing with demanding customers has occasionally been unpleasant. Wanting more children and having difficulty conceiving them has been very frustrating. But overall, King says that life has been very good to him. He is not famous within business circles. The Prime Minister of Canada is unlikely to call on him for advice. He cannot make a decision to spend a billion dollars on an acquisition or to fire 10,000 people. But in 1993, he is the president of his own firm. He has no boss, a wife and two children, a beautiful house, a large income, and an equity stake in his company worth many millions of dollars. It is not a bad life.

---

The public links successful HBS graduates with top management jobs in large industrial companies. The two best-known members of the Class of '49, for example, are Jim Burke and Peter Mc-Colough. Burke capped his career as Chairman of Johnson & Johnson; McColough as Chairman of Xerox. Against that standard, Jeremy King is clearly an oddity. But is he?

Big businesses like those once run by Jim Burke and Peter Mc-Colough are linked in people's minds to business schools for very good reasons. Neither existed a century and a half ago. Both grew up together, and for the most part, in a mutually beneficial relationship (see historical discussion on the next page). At Harvard, this relationship was and is very visible. For decades the press has talked about HBS MBAs as if they were captains of ocean liners or aircraft carriers. On campus, the big business presence starts with the physical plant itself. The library is named after Baker (Citicorp). The MBA classroom building is named after Aldrich/Rockefeller (Standard Oil). The dining hall is Kresge (K-Mart). One executive program has classes in Cumnock (J. P. Stevens). The faculty office building is Morgan (Morgan Guaranty, Morgan Stanley). Guest speakers in a typical year might include the heads of P & G, General Motors, G.E., Chemical Bank, IBM, and so on. During recruiting season, the list of interviewers on campus includes those firms plus dozens of other well-known and sizable corporations.

And all of this makes Exhibit 2.1 particularly interesting. Despite the fact that small and very small organizations were almost invisible in the formal on-campus placement process in the spring of 1974, fully 28% of that year's MBA graduating class somehow got jobs with these firms. Only a few more, about 36%, took jobs with large or very large organizations. The rest went to medium-

## BUSINESS SCHOOLS AND BIG BUSINESS

Before 1860, most businesses had an owner, or an owner with a few assistants, who directed a very small number of employees.[1] The office setting in Dickens's *A Christmas Carol*, with businessman Ebenezer Scrooge and employee Bob Cratchit, was commonplace. For all practical purposes, large firms, managerial hierarchies, and modern managers did not exist in the United States until the last half of the 19th century. But then, in a relatively short period of time, firms grew in size and thousands of managerial jobs were created. At first, the owners' assistants became managers, as did some of the workers. But as businesses became more complex, so did the managerial jobs. Complaints can be found as early as the 1860s that firms were having trouble finding enough people qualified for these new positions.[2]

In 1881, the University of Pennsylvania responded to these events by founding the Wharton School of Finance and Commerce, which offered an undergraduate degree in business management. California and Chicago set up business schools seventeen years later, followed by a few others, and then in 1908, by Harvard.[3] Unlike Pennsylvania, Chicago, et al., Harvard offered a masters degree in business administration. Using its law school as a model, it sought young men who already had finished their undergraduate education. The School hoped to make them professional managers who could handle the complex duties in the increasing number of medium- and large-sized businesses. George Baker, the head of what today is Citicorp, was so impressed by what he saw that in 1925 he gave the School money to construct an entire eight building campus.[4]

By 1926, a total of 57,728 students were majoring in business subjects at 132 U.S. colleges and universities. A total of 2,575 faculty members taught business courses. In their report of a study of management education conducted at about that time, two Wharton professors state explicitly where the participants in these programs were going: "It is clear that a preponderance and increasing proportion of management business graduates will enter the employ of large enterprises."[5] In the 1930s, '40s, '50s, and '60s, the most visibly successful graduates of management schools did just that. They went to big business and (like Burke and McColough) eventually became CEOs.

A mutually beneficial relationship developed between many business schools and large firms. Harvard received donations from big corporations to support its programs and research. It also obtained access to study interesting business problems and to write teaching cases. The first major piece of social science research conducted by professors at HBS was possible only with the cooperation of a Western Electric (AT&T) factory in the Chicago area.[6] In return, the School trained people to assume managerial careers in big companies and helped those businesses to gain access to students through an on-campus lecture series and a job placement program.

Small businesses were mostly left out of this relationship. They were not in the job market for young managers every year. They had little money to donate to HBS. Besides, they wanted street-smart generalists more than the analytical specialists who tend to be the product of universities.

sized firms.* But this surprisingly low employment rate in big business was, in fact, just the beginning of a long-term trend downward. By 1983 only 31% of the Class of '74 were in big business. In 1991, only 23%. At the other extreme, small business accounted for 43% of those graduates in 1983 and a whopping 62% in 1992. Jeremy King's employment in a small business is anything but an oddity.

EXHIBIT 2.1

### Size of Employers for Graduates of Harvard's MBA Class of 1974

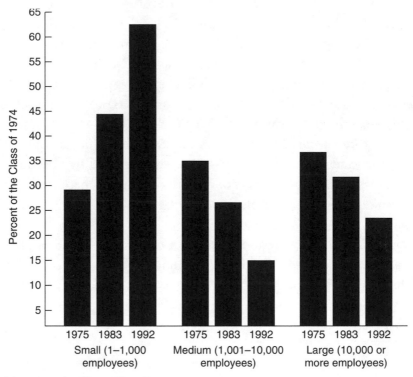

For more detail, see Note 7.

---

*Very small = 1–100 employees, small = 101–1,000, medium = 1,001–10,000, large = 10,001–100,000, and very large = 100,001 or more.

Responses to questionnaires from other HBS groups attending their 15th and 20th reunions strongly suggest that the information in Exhibit 2.1 is not idiosyncratic to the Class of '74. Although students from the 1930s and '40s appear to have gone mainly to big business, more recent MBAs have increasingly turned to small businesses.[8] In the Class of '59, for example, about 65% were in small firms at their 30th reunion.[9] If current trends continue, 75% or more of the Class of '74 might be in small businesses by their 30th reunion. In light of Harvard's history, curriculum, relationship with big business, and placement process, this pattern is almost the equivalent of West Point graduates no longer pursuing careers in the military.

---

When Kevin Johnson, Jeremy King, and their colleagues were first-year MBA students, they all took a course called "Organizational Problems." In thirty sessions, they studied twenty-nine business cases, only one of which was about an entrepreneur. Such a skewed ratio of publicly owned and professionally run situations to entrepreneurial situations was similar in most of the required courses and was perfectly consistent with the School's big business focus. If there was a subliminal message in much of the curriculum, it was that entrepreneurs were unsophisticated and entrepreneurial contexts were unworthy of the powerful analytical tools being taught. One did not need an MBA from a prestigious institution to supervise "car hawkers" at a Chevy dealer or "hamburger flippers" at a McDonald's franchise. A successful MBA was a professional who ran a complex enterprise. At least one book by an HBS faculty member was quite explicit about this point: the School was not trying to produce the "promoter/entrepreneur," but instead the "administrator/manager."[10]

Out of a total of forty-two elective courses in 1973–1974, the School did offer two that focused on small businesses and that often looked at entrepreneurial situations. But almost none of the regular faculty wanted to teach these courses, partially because entrepreneurship was not a business school specialty with any prestige, and partially because it was not seen as central to the School's mission. More often than not, the courses were turned over to adjunct or visiting professors.

Even the School's educational process felt more like a publicly owned corporation than an entrepreneurial business. Structure and regimentation were commonplace. Each day, day after day, students read about three business situations and then met with the same group of eighty other classmates to discuss those cases. There was little room for individual initiative. The HBS bureaucracy fed them, housed them, educated them, and generally told them what to do and when to do it. Suggestions from students were sometimes greeted by the administration with all the enthusiasm of the most entrenched civil servant in the U.S. Postal Service.

Phil Morin liked most of what he found at HBS, but hated the regimentation. Entrepreneurial by nature, he found the business school experience painful at times, not because of the long hours and hard work, but because of what he perceived as a prison-like atmosphere. He thought seriously about dropping out, but refused to accept that he could be defeated.

At the end of his educational experience, Morin found almost no entrepreneurs came to campus offering jobs. The placement process was built almost entirely around the likes of Citicorp and W. R. Grace. Firms full of professional managers, some of them with MBAs, came to Boston to hire more of the same. This pattern is entirely consistent with most people's perception of HBS and its graduates. Most assume these MBAs are professionally trained individuals who end up running the enterprises built by self-taught men and women like Sam Walton, Tom Watson, Sr., and Mary Kay Ash. The idea is that once the original entrepreneurs are gone and the business is big, one needs the more sophisticated and systemic talents of the MBA.

All this makes the figures shown in Exhibit 2.2 very interesting. A large percentage of the Class of '74 are working outside of the confines of publicly owned corporations. Many have started their

EXHIBIT 2.2

Entrepreneurs from Harvard's
MBA Class of '74

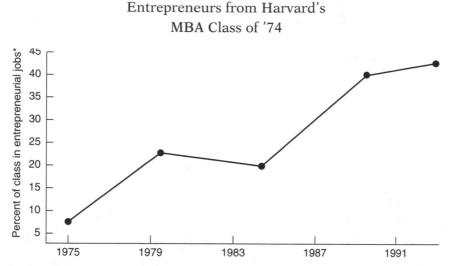

*Individuals who own and run, or partially own and help run, a business as their primary job. Does not include people who are retired, unemployed, or no longer in MBA-like careers (e.g., writer).

own businesses. Some have obtained significant equity stakes and top management positions in businesses started by others. A few are self-employed. But in total, over 40% of the Class in 1992 are entrepreneurs of some sort. Over 40%. Even more are behaving in an entrepreneurial way by negotiating significant business deals or providing leadership to grow businesses—around 70% of the class.

In 1973, if you had told young Assistant Professor Kotter (yours truly) that close to half of his students would eventually become entrepreneurs, he probably would have probably given you the condescending smile that academics reserve for the uneducated and the uninformed.[11]

In their "Organizational Problems" course, students discussed cases in both manufacturing and nonmanufacturing settings, but not in equal numbers. About eighteen of the situations involved manufacturing firms, including cases on TRW, Alcon Laboratories, Continental Can (called "Empire Glass"), ITT, Clark Equipment, Inland Steel (called "Continental Steel"), a large petroleum company ("Texana"), a sportswear firm ("Samantha"), two electronics companies ("Higgins Equipment" and "Baines Electronics"), and an aerospace firm ("Aerospace Systems"). Nine cases were in non-manufacturing, including ones on Stop and Shop supermarkets ("Randley Stores"), a limo/taxi/rental transportation company ("Denver Transportation"), and a trading organization ("International Metals"). This pattern was also common in the required curriculum. The marketing course focused on marketing products. The operations course focused almost exclusively on manufacturing. Accounting and control classes usually stayed within the confines of industrial businesses. Role models for success were mostly senior executives in manufacturing firms. When asked to justify all this, faculty noted that it simply reflected both what was important and that in which the United States excelled: the Fortune 500. Students were taught how to market products like Procter & Gamble and how to build products like Ford.

The placement process and the on-campus lecture series had more non-manufacturing representatives than the curriculum. Some commercial banks (like Citicorp and First Chicago), consulting firms (like McKinsey), and investment banks (Goldman Sachs) were very active. But manufacturing was still the norm.

The career path statistics for the Class of '74 are again interesting (see Exhibit 2.3). Fewer graduates began their jobs in manufacturing than one would have expected from all the signals at HBS; for every student who took a position at graduation with a manufacturing company, two took jobs elsewhere. Fewer still were in manufacturing in 1991—only about 21% of the class.

Those in non-manufacturing are employed in a variety of different industries. The biggest single concentration is in finance—commercial banking, investment banking, investment management, and trading—accounting for about 31% of the Class in 1991. Another 10% are in consulting and 7% are in real estate. About 5% are in distribution.

EXHIBIT 2.3

Industries in Which the MBAs
From Harvard's Class of '74 Work

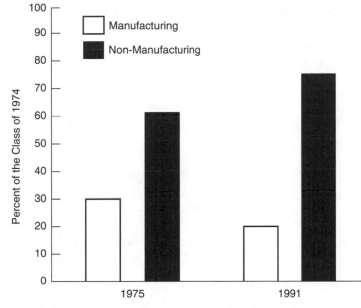

Does not include people who are retired, unemployed, or no longer in MBA-like careers (e.g., writer).

This trend away from manufacturing is interrelated with the trends to small business and entrepreneurial situations. There is simply a much higher percentage of manufacturing businesses among big publicly owned firms than among small or closely held companies.

In combination, these three trends mean that very few people are pursuing careers in the tradition of Jim Burke and Peter Mc-Colough. In 1992, only about 8% of the Class of '74 were either executives in manufacturing firms or well on their way to these positions. *Eight percent.* And that includes manufacturing firms of all sizes. Nearly half (48%) are entrepreneurs or are very actively trying to become entrepreneurs. Another 29% are executives in non-manufacturing firms (or close to becoming that). The rest are solidly in middle management (8%) or are no longer pursuing MBA careers (9%, including those who are retired or in the military).

Jeremy King is not an oddity in the class. Fellow '74 graduate Ralph Dunhill is the executive vice president of an industrial firm with over $5 billion in revenues. Ralph is the oddity.

---

Why are they following non-traditional career paths? We will explore this issue in some detail in Chapters 3 through 7. For now, I

EXHIBIT 2.4

Income Differentials Between Class of '74 MBAs
That Have Pursued Traditional versus Non-traditional Careers

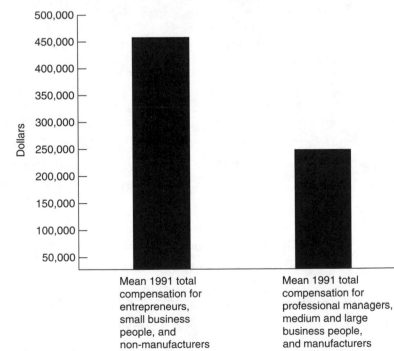

For more detail, see Note 12.

can only say that the succinct answer is: that is where the bigger opportunities lie.

It is revealing to look at those in the class who have crafted traditional careers as professional managers, often in large firms, especially large manufacturing firms. By many measures, most of those people have been significantly less successful than their more unconventional classmates (see Exhibits 2.4 and 2.5). As we will see throughout this book, the traditionalists on average earn less money. They typically have less real power or authority. And they often report either facing more problems or receiving less personal satisfaction from their work.

Furthermore, I have been increasingly encountering throughout the workplace what we see here in one MBA class. Many careers that served individuals well for much of this century no longer

EXHIBIT 2.5

Power/Autonomy Differentials Between Those Class of '74 MBAs That Followed Conventional versus Unconventional Careers

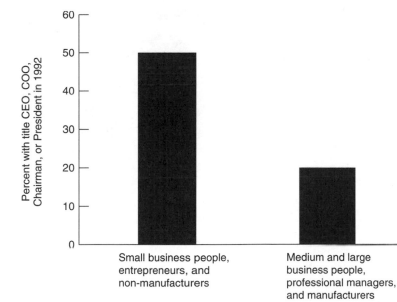

For more detail, see Note 13.

seem to be the source of great opportunity. This would include not only executive careers in big industrial enterprises, but also union careers in those same organizations. Very powerful forces are changing life at work—for top executives, unskilled workers, and just about everyone else.

---

### NEW RULE #1

The location of opportunities is shifting. Succeeding at work today demands strategies and career paths that are often different from mid-20th century norms. Increasingly, the new rule is: beware of the conventional and traditional. In a time of rapid change, the unconventional often wins.

---

# 3

---

# THE POST '73 ECONOMIC
# ENVIRONMENT

---

To understand why traditional careers in Fortune 500 firms are not paying off as much as they did a few decades ago, one needs to appreciate how the economy has been changing. The business world of today is significantly different from the one that existed for most of this century. In particular, a comparison of 1994 to 1954 shows a major shift in competitiveness that has changed the rules of the game in virtually all industries and in most countries.

---

The single date which best separates the economic era after World War II from the one in which we currently live is probably October 16, 1973.[1] On that day, Gulf State oil producers for the first time raised the posted price of petroleum both unilaterally and significantly—up 70% to $5.11 a barrel despite massive protests from Western oil companies. On October 17, Arab oil ministers agreed to cut back production, driving some bids by mid-December up to $17.00 a barrel.[2] These two actions, more than any other, signaled the end of U.S. economic dominance in the world and the beginning of a truly globalized economy.*

Kevin Johnson and his classmates experienced the immediate aftershock of these decisions in much the same way as most Americans. Because some Boston car owners panicked, long lines could occasionally be found at two nearby filling stations on the corner of North Harvard Street and Western Avenue. Ray Collins shakes his head when he remembers waiting an hour to get gas and seeing some people pump only four or five gallons before their tanks were full. Like other Americans, economists, business people, and even public policy experts, few of our MBAs seems to have recognized the total significance of these events. Nor did many foresee the eventual irony—that actions designed to limit competition, regulate prices, and create stability for oil producers would mark the beginning of an economic era characterized by more competition, less regulation, and more instability.

This new era can be conceived as the third phase of big company capitalism in the United States.[3] Phase I ran from about 1860 to 1930, roughly three generations, going from Class of '74 great-grandparents through the birth of their parents. During this time, the first truly big businesses were created in the United States. Much that is good is associated with this period; life expectancy and incomes generally rose a great deal. But there was also a dark side to this era; abuses of new corporate power were troubling and the distance between the rich and poor grew (see historical discussion on next page). Driven by the Industrial Revolution and guided by Republican presidents, Phase I was replaced

---

*Although there were events between the end of World War II and 1973 in which the United States was humbled politically and/or militarily, no actions taken by people outside the U.S. had the economic effect of the first oil shock. 1973 shattered any notion that the U.S. economy was so strong that it was basically invulnerable to economic forces elsewhere in the world.

## PHASE I OF BIG COMPANY CAPITALISM
## IN THE UNITED STATES

This was an era in which the very first large American business enterprises were created—U.S. Steel, Standard Oil, General Motors, General Electric.[4] At one level, the Civil War was a struggle between people who wanted to remain agrarian and feudal versus others who wanted to capitalize on the Industrial Revolution. Industrialism won and then blossomed under the guidance of the Republican party, the winner of thirteen of seventeen Presidential elections during this period. In this era, thousands and thousands of manufacturing enterprises were launched and an unprecedented number of inventions and important scientific discoveries were made. Burroughs created the first modern adding machine, Westinghouse the air brake, Carrier the air conditioner, Sperry the automatic airline pilot, Eastman the camera, Birdseye the process of freezing food, Schick the electric razor, and Bell the telephone. Between 1880 and 1930, more important innovations were developed in the United States than in any other fifty year period, in any country, before or since.[5]

By many standards, Phase I of big company capitalism was a huge success. Life expectancy rose from about thirty-nine years to nearly sixty.[6] Labor-saving inventions made work much less physically burdensome. Millions of people whose ancestors had always been among the rural poor now moved into the middle class. By 1925, many people lived a life that was not even a dream for their great-grandparents.

Nevertheless, with all the good came much that was undesirable. Industrialism caused massive change and disruption in lives and communities. Some factory owners and managers used their new economic power to exploit workers with long hours and unsafe conditions. Economic cycles of expansion and depression created much hardship. Most troublesome of all, in a social sense, was the growing gap between the rich and the poor. Even the least wealthy improved their lot. But the distance between the average citizen and the top—now represented not by a large landowner but an industrialist like Rockefeller—grew to gargantuan levels.

around 1930 by a new period that was heavily influenced by government action guided by the Democrats. Running from about 1930 to 1970, an era in which the Democratic party won seven of ten Presidential elections, Phase II attempted to ameliorate the problems of big company capitalism without abandoning capitalism itself.

The prelude to this second era came at the beginning of the century with antitrust legislation and a constitutional amendment allowing income taxes. But the death of Phase I required 1929's Black Tuesday, the Great Depression, and thus the destruction of the credibility of that form of laissez-faire capitalism. With Roosevelt and the New Deal came an unprecedented amount of government intervention into the economy designed to curb boom/bust cycles and reduce the economic gap between the rich and poor. Keynesian economics was first applied in a major way. The Social Security Act of 1935 helped transfer wealth from the rich to the poor, as did income tax increases (which pushed the highest marginal rate in 1944 to 94%) and the 1935 Wagner Act (which helped push union membership from 11.6% of the total non-agricultural work force in 1930 to over 30% at the end of World War II). Other regulations in the 1930s, '40s, '50s, and '60s tried in hundreds of different ways to achieve similar ends: to reduce the problems created by modern economic competition by stimulating the economy during downturns, by regulating corporate and managerial behavior, by helping the poor to compete in the labor market through education and organization, and by providing income to those who could not compete. Even some policies in large corporations had a very similar effect. Corporate bureaucracy limited the kind of speculation and risk taking that helped create booms and busts. Compensation and salary policies limited the range of income from janitor to CEO.*

Like Phase I, this second era of big company capitalism was enormously successful by many measures. Life expectancy continued to

---

*This was the era, for example, in which Hay and other compensation systems were invented.

rise, going from 59.7 to 70.8.[7] By today's standards, people living in poverty fell from over 40% of the population to just 12.6%.[8] From the end of World War II until 1973, real wages of production workers in the United States grew a solid $2\frac{1}{2}$ to 3% each year.[9] Boom-bust cycles became much less severe. Conveniences and sources of entertainment, once available only to the rich, became accessible to nearly everyone. This included not only washing machines and televisions, but even the mighty automobile and airplane.

But just as the beginnings of big company capitalism had a dark side, so did Phase II. Literally millions and millions of rules from government, labor unions, and corporations limited competition and created huge bureaucracies which were somewhat slow, expensive, and inefficient. By the end of Phase II, millions of "professional managers" and their "workers" had learned to accept this system as normal and good. The consequences were relatively invisible as long as corporations competed only against other corporations operating in a similar way and in a similar context, or as long as they were competing only against much weaker foreign firms. When there were only GM, Ford, Chrysler, and American Motors, few noticed that they all had signed contracts with the United Auto Workers Union that unnecessarily increased the cost of cars or that they all had bureaucracies that were slow to respond to consumer preferences and new technological possibilities. But people did notice when gasoline suddenly tripled in price and firms from Japan quickly responded to this change by offering more efficient and less expensive cars.

As Phase I was influenced heavily by the Industrial Revolution and Phase II by government action, Phase III appears to be mostly the product of increasing globalization.* A part of this shows in

---

*Some would say that techonological change is again the primary driving force. Globalization and technology changes are clearly feeding each other. Increased globalization means increasing competition, which in turn is stimulating investment in R&D, which in turn is increasing the rate of technological change, which in some cases (e.g., faxes, Concordes) is increasing globalization.

trade figures, where the United States expanded exports and imports by 500% between 1973 and 1991 while Japan saw a 700% jump.[10] But globalization means much more than trade. Geographically distant parts of the earth have been becoming more and more related since the early 1500s, but only recently have we seen the possibility of a small group of people making an economic decision that immediately has consequences to billions of people and thousands of corporations spread over the entire world.

Globalization is the product of many forces, some of which are political (no major war since 1945), some of which are technological (faster and cheaper transportation and communication), and some of which are economic (mature firms seeking growth outside their national boundaries). Increased global economic interdependence has disrupted systems of social welfare capitalism in the U.S. and Europe, shaken rigid structures of state ownership and family capitalism in the developing world, and helped destroy Communism in the Soviet Union and Eastern Europe. It has also had a devastating effect on the global market share of a number of U.S. industries.*

EXHIBIT 3.1

Stages of Big Company Capitalism in the U.S.

| Phase I | Phase II | Phase III |
|---|---|---|
| • Key influence: The Industrial Revolution | • Key influence: Government action | • Key influence: The globalization of markets and competition |
| • Mostly Republican administrations in Washington | • Mostly Democratic administrations in Washington | • Mostly Republican administrations in Washington thus far |

1860 ——————▶1930 ———————▶ 1970 ——————————▶

---

*For example: in tires, the decline has been from 35% to 24%.[11] In steel, the decline has been from 19% to 12%.[12] In TVs, the decline has been from 17% to 12%.[13] In autos, the decline has been from 28% to 17%.[14]

In 1973, anyone who would have predicted all this change would have been ignored or ridiculed. Today, most people are generally aware of these trends, but I think very few have thought clearly about what all this implies. The implications are many and very significant—especially regarding what it takes to succeed at work today and why so many in the Class of '74 are pursuing careers outside of professional management in Fortune 500 firms.

---

The response almost everywhere to this new economic era has been to reluctantly shed rules, regulations, bureaucracy, and bureaucratic mind-sets in order to better compete. In the United States thus far, this has come under the guiding hand of mostly Republican administrations in Washington.* In general, actions have come slowly, often painfully, and with major consequences for nearly everyone—including young and well-educated individuals like Michael Lender from the Class of '74.

Michael was born in Tennessee in 1948, the third child of a pharmaceutical salesman and an office secretary. He did well but not outstanding in high school, attended Western Reserve University in Cleveland, and received a bachelor's degree in 1970 in accounting, a subject he admits to both loving and hating. For two years, he worked for Price Waterhouse in Cleveland before coming to graduate school in Boston. In 1974, he rejoined that large auditing firm in Cleveland, but stayed for only a year. In October 1975, he accepted an employment offer from one of his large manufacturing clients to work in their corporate accounting office.

"When I arrived" Michael reports in a slight southern drawl that he still has in 1994, "Chicago Industrials had already experienced competition from Europe and the Far East. But that increased a whole lot in 1975 and 1976—partially because CI passed on in

---

*As I write this in May 1993, the Democrats have been in the White House only $4^1/_2$ of the last $24^1/_4$ years.

creased energy costs to their customers while a Japanese competitor very aggressively altered production processes to make them less dependent on expensive oil. As a result, our revenue growth slowed, and our profitability decreased along with market share. Senior management initiated only minor responses to all this until about 1979. Then they turned for help to a consulting firm which employed one of my classmates, Trevor James" (see profile on the next page).

After a year-long study, the consultants recommended a number of significant changes at Lender's firm. "They argued that one business should be sold because the company had no sustainable competitive advantages that would help it win over the long term," Michael later recalled. "They recommended a major reorganization designed mostly to reduce headquarters staff and the accompanying bureaucracy. They suggested that the firm's unions needed to be confronted about the new competitive realities and that restrictive work rules be significantly reduced. They also identified three acquisition possibilities which would increase market share and global reach in two central business areas."

The consultant's recommendations were backed by reasonably tight logic and a great deal of quantitative data. Michael was impressed: "In an MBA program, the report would have received an A." Most of the firm's management gave it a C–. The arguments against significant change were endless: results were not poor enough to justify risky actions, the consultants were young and inexperienced and did not know the firm's businesses, the Japanese competition had been more lucky than smart, confronting the unions was naive and dangerous, the business marked for divestiture was basically sound and could be made into a winner, the reorganization would strip away muscle as well as fat, and on and on. After nearly fifty years of success, the firm's corporate culture was simply unable to deal with the new competitive situation. In this and many other respects, its situation was far from unique.[15]

Three years elapsed, results got worse, and two key players in top management retired early. Then, after much discussion, be-

# TREVOR JAMES

PROFESSIONAL

1986–1993    The Gordon-James Consulting Group, Washington, D.C.
- Co-founder and President

1974–1985    Wallace Evers (a large consulting firm),
Washington, D.C.
- Principal (1985)
- Practice Leader (1984)
- Senior Consultant (1980-1984)
- Consultant (1974-1979)

1968–1972    United Air Lines, Chicago

EDUCATION

1972–1974    Harvard Business School, Boston, MA

1964–1968    University of Massachusetts, Boston, MA
B.S. in Aerospace Engineering. Chairman of "Arts and World Affairs Committee," member of varsity swimming team, and editor of school magazine.

PERSONAL

Born in Boston, 1944. Second of six children. Father was an independent electrician, mother was not employed outside the home.

Married Helen Dugan, 1973. Four children, ages 15, 13, 10, and 6. Helen has an MBA and also works for Gordon-James.

Quote: "After coming out of that pressure cooker environment at Wallace Evers, I started to take the time to unwind and look around me. My perception of success was defined by the people I dealt with, so that meant being an executive in a big corporation. When I got out of there and I started to look around, I realized that the guy who owns three Midas muffler shops makes very good money. Maybe he is not really well educated, but if you start talking to this guy, you realize that there are a lot of ways to live your life, and a lot of interesting people in the world who are doing it differently from you. (1991)"

tween 1983 and 1987 most of the consultant's ideas were implemented. As a result, Michael's former job in corporate accounting
and hundreds of other staff positions were eliminated. One business was sold and four others were purchased. After a brief strike,
restrictive work practices and high wage levels were rolled back,
affecting thousands of union members. The union gave in only because it was on the defensive everywhere, like most of the U.S.
labor movement. In 1970, 28.4% of the U.S. non-agricultural labor
force was unionized. By 1991, that figure had fallen to 16.1%.[16]

The sweeping changes the firm made in the mid-1980s affected
all employees. Promotion within the managerial hierarchy stopped
coming to those who were traditional, bureaucratic managers. Increasingly, getting ahead required the leadership capacity to build
or turn around businesses. Some people found these changes confusing and very threatening. Others, like Michael, viewed events in
a different way. "The changes in our industry certainly have been
frustrating at times," he reported in a 1984 interview, "but they
have also been very exciting. I hate being bored—that's what finally happened to me with accounting. Although the last six or
seven years have not always been fun, they surely haven't been
boring."

Michael moved out of the corporate accounting job in 1977. "I
was being stereotyped as a bean counter because of my background and I decided the only way to break that was to get out of
accounting." He worked for two years in a distribution job. "Then
the first consultants were in and I tried to get a position where I
could act on some of their ideas. I eventually succeeded in getting
that kind of job, began implementing some of their concepts, and
then discovered that many people in top management hated the
consulting report." For twelve months his career at CI seemed to
die. When he heard rumors that he would be transferred back to
corporate accounting, he began looking for jobs elsewhere. "Then
some changes occurred in senior management, and suddenly I
was no longer an outcast. I was even asked what I wanted next,
and I told them I wanted to run a division. They said I wasn't

ready, but nine months later I got a big promotion to run one of the smaller and newer businesses."

Between 1985 and 1989, Lender's division grew by nearly 70%. "It was an amazing time. Because CI was going through so many changes, corporate headquarters was more of a distraction than an asset to us. And our competition got tougher too. But we did some relatively innovative things, got lucky in a few cases, and did well. Overall, it was a stressful but excellent experience for me. If I had been born twenty years earlier, I would probably not have gotten a division general manager's job at such a young age or the superb experience in that job. I also would never have received or accepted an offer to be president of one of our increasingly important distributors (see profile on the next page). In my father's generation, at this stage in my career I probably at best would be the VP of accounting at a place like Chicago Industrials instead of the CEO of a small firm."

This pattern is seen throughout Class of '74 experiences. A more volatile business environment creates problems and opportunities for people, changing what is rewarded and who gets ahead. People like Michael Lender have found ways to use this to their advantage in career paths that are often different from those of successful executives in their parents' generation.

---

When Harold Atkins joined an investment banking firm in 1976, he never seriously considered an offer to work in their bond trading group. Bonds were boring and bond traders made less money than most of their colleagues. But then on October 5, 1979, Federal Reserve Chairman Paul Volcker announced policy changes that allowed interest rates to be more volatile. In a sense, he took out a few more bolts in the huge regulatory machine that built up in the 1930s, '40s, '50s, '60s, and early '70s. One of the consequences of this action was that bond prices, always closely tied to

# MICHAEL LENDER

### PRX Services, Minneapolis, Minnesota (1990–1993)

- President and COO

### Chicago Industrials, Chicago, Illinois (1975–1989)

- General Manager, LDX Division (1985–1989)
- V.P. of Administration, Phiro Division (1980–1984)
- Director of Distribution, Phiro Division (1978–1979)
- Corporate Accounting Staff (1975–1977)

### Price Waterhouse, Cleveland, Ohio (1970–1972)

- Accountant

### Western Reserve University, Cleveland, Ohio

Received B.S. in Accounting, 1970. Member of College Bowl team and chairperson of "Acting in the Community Together" program.

### PERSONAL

Married Louise Walcott in 1977. Three children.

### QUOTE

"Raising a child with a serious learning disability has been exasperating at times, but it also has taught me a great deal about the world and myself, and it has drawn me closer to my family. (1984)"

interest rates, began to fluctuate more widely. When bond prices move slowly, it is difficult to make a killing in the bond market. When they move fast, one can make or lose a lot of money, and anyone good at bond trading can command a better salary.

Incomes of bond traders went up for another reason as well. When the United States lost its dominant world economic position and was forced to compete against some tough global players, corporate and government and personal borrowing skyrocketed. Total debt went from $323 billion in 1977 to $7 trillion in 1985. With their profitability often reduced,* corporations loaded up with debt to help them restructure to become more competitive and, in some cases, to make them less attractive as acquisition candidates. Individuals added debt so they could continue to spend when their incomes no longer kept up with their expectations. Since government revenues are closely linked to corporate and personal income, the government loaded up with debt to pay its ever-rising bills, a part of which was coming from an intensified military competition with the USSR. A great deal of the combined corporate, personal, and government debt was in the form of bonds. As a result, a trader that handled $5 million per week in bonds in 1975 might actually have dealt $300 million per day in 1985.[18] Since income tends to be tied to volume, salaries went up and up.† Because Harold Atkins spotted this trend relatively early and was able to develop an entrepreneurial attitude, he managed to switch into bonds and make a bundle.

Freddie Lowe experienced another version of the same phenomenon. In the spring of 1974, he had to decide whether to go into a

---

*Corporate profits were 11.7% of GNP in the mid-1960s (adjusted for inventory gains and losses and for depreciation). By the late 1980s, a comparable figure was 5.3%.[17]

†Stock brokers also saw their incomes go up with a great increase in stock trading volume. The precise factors fueling bond and stock trading are different but both are linked to the emergence of a Phase III economic environment.

small, low-tech, family business. This firm had been founded by his grandfather during Phase I of U.S. big business capitalism (1906). After poor performance in 1932, 1933, and 1934, the company grew slowly but steadily under his father's guidance during Phase II. Freddie assumed that if he joined the firm, he would enjoy a good income as had his father. But he feared he would run the risk of boredom, forgo the chances of getting really rich, and have to fight his father to gain any significant authority. Two of Freddie's undergraduate fraternity brothers had faced similar situations a few years before and had gone the family business route. After much thought, and with some reservations, Freddie followed suit. The three young men believed they would be peers and friends for a lifetime, enjoying a quality of life symbolized by membership in the Union Club. It has not worked out that way.

Although for different reasons, in all three cases the industries became much more volatile in the late 1970s. Each firm reacted differently. One continued operations pretty much as in the past. The other two became more aggressive, selling product lines and buying new businesses. The firm that did not change much ended up in trouble and was eventually sold at a low price. One of the two that tried to change also ended up in trouble, mostly because of some bad strategic decisions and too much debt. The third did incredibly well—growing from $10 million per year in revenues to over $100 million in one decade. Guided by very able leadership, this business drove down costs by increasing productivity with information technology and then increased its market share dramatically through lower prices. As a result, one of the young men in 1993 was making $50,000 per year, had a net worth of $200,000, and was not particularly happy. A second had income of $90,000 and wealth of $650,000. The third was making $250,000, had an equity interest in his firm worth over $10,000,000, loved his job, and by most objective standards was making a very useful contribution to his community.* The latter was Freddie.

---

*The contribution took many forms, including creating an increasing number of jobs and providing significant gifts to local charities.

As it affects opportunities, the net result of recent economic changes has been threefold. First, the sheer increase in global competition has, at least for now, greatly slowed wage growth in the United States. In many jobs, wage increases have not kept up with inflation since 1974. Second, the distance between the highest- and lowest-paying jobs has grown. This is not an unusual outcome when the level of competition increases, especially when market size also grows. Third, the location of the biggest opportunities has shifted: away from large bureaucratic companies to smaller or more entrepreneurial ones, away from some manufacturing to some non-manufacturing industries, and away from professional management to entrepreneurial, leadership, and deal-maker roles (see Exhibit 3.2).

In a Phase II economy, the managerial skills associated with large and publicly owned U.S. manufacturing enterprises were rewarded handsomely. In Phase III, this is often not true. In Phase III, the more competitive and faster-moving business environment has been tough on firms that are bureaucratic and inwardly focused.* Economies of huge scale, the prime competitive strategy used in Phases I and II by many big businesses, are no longer working as well in a world marketplace with too much production capacity and with technology that increasingly allows small units to be cost-effective (e.g. with microprocessors).† In some big busi-

---

*For example, the percent of the U.S. working population employed in Fortune 500 firms rose from 14.6% in 1954 to 19.4% in 1974. Since then, the movement has been away from these large industrial companies. In 1992 only 10.9% of the working population were in Fortune 500 firms.[19]

†As Robert Reich has pointed out, "firms that are surviving and succeeding are shifting from high volume to high value." This strategy works better today "because customers are willing to pay a premium for goods and services that exactly meet their needs and because the high value business cannot easily be duplicated by high volume competition around the world."[20]

EXHIBIT 3.2

The Effect of the Post 1973 Economic
Environment on Industries, Firms, and Careers

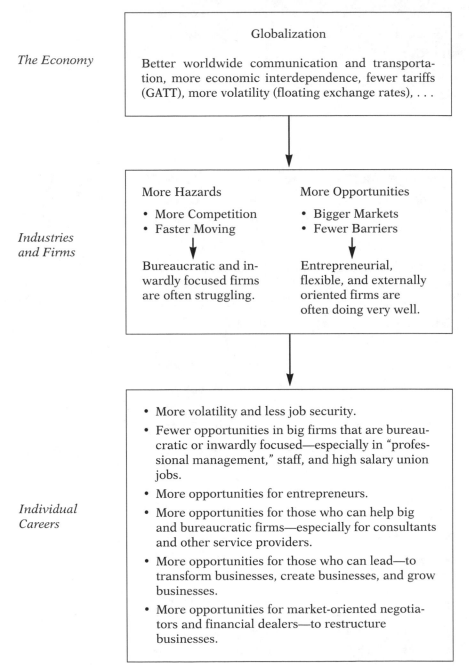

*The Economy*

**Globalization**

Better worldwide communication and transportation, more economic interdependence, fewer tariffs
(GATT), more volatility (floating exchange rates), . . .

*Industries
and Firms*

More Hazards

- More Competition
- Faster Moving

Bureaucratic and in-
wardly focused firms
are often struggling.

More Opportunities

- Bigger Markets
- Fewer Barriers

Entrepreneurial,
flexible, and externally
oriented firms are
often doing very well.

*Individual
Careers*

- More volatility and less job security.
- Fewer opportunities in big firms that are bureaucratic or inwardly focused—especially in "professional management," staff, and high salary union
  jobs.
- More opportunities for entrepreneurs.
- More opportunities for those who can help big
  and bureaucratic firms—especially for consultants
  and other service providers.
- More opportunities for those who can lead—to
  transform businesses, create businesses, and grow
  businesses.
- More opportunities for market-oriented negotiators and financial dealers—to restructure
  businesses.

nesses, gigantic size has even created diseconomies of scale. Smaller firms have rarely been able to compete with an economies of scale strategy; they have traditionally been forced to go the high-value route. As a result, smaller firms, usually leaner and more flexible and more customer focused, have fared much better recently than giants. Accounting for virtually all the job growth in the United States in the last twenty years, small companies now often tend to offer more opportunities than large enterprises, especially for good entrepreneurial leaders and wheeler-dealers. And the biggest opportunities of all today, along with big risks, come from not just helping to run a small business, but from owning a significant piece of it too. As a general rule, the more wide open the business environment, the more entrepreneurial opportunities there will be, and Phase III is much more open than was Phase II. Some statistics make the point dramatically; while 93,000 corporations were created in the United States in 1950, by the late 1980s the number had grown to 1.3 million per year.[21]

These changes have affected everyone, not just baby boomers, but also their parents and even the oldest children of the post-World War II generation. So far, many have not benefited from these shifts. A few have been hurt a great deal—often precisely those who benefited the most from Phase II: relatively unskilled and uneducated individuals working in large industrial enterprises.* The problems encountered by some older union workers in manufacturing firms have been massive. After being laid off, senior union members have often discovered that they have few relevant skills to

---

*The second phase of big company capitalism in the United States succeeded in reducing the distance between people's incomes.[22] As competition increases in Phase III, and as more and more of the Phase II regulating machinery is jettisoned, the income gap is growing again between rich and poor, poor and very poor, rich and very rich.[23] And just as at the beginning of the 20th century, some people are now becoming more and more concerned about this trend and its implications.[24]

offer employers and that the market rates for these skills are not even remotely close to their previous salaries.[25] Even non-unionized middle level managers in these same large businesses have sometimes found, after being laid off, that the labor market does not value their skills highly either. One commonly hears today reports of unemployed middle managers being forced to take 10–30% pay cuts in order to regain employment.

Of course, not everyone has been hurt by all these changes. The number of millionaires and billionaires has grown rapidly in the past fifteen years, and not just in the United States.* In an era of larger and more open markets, some people have found significantly more economic opportunities than were available to their parents and grandparents. Some of these individuals have been exceptionally successful at capitalizing on these new opportunities. The most visible of this group tend to be entertainers and sports stars. Bill Cosby and Jack Nicholson have each made more money in the past decade than dozens of movie stars made collectively in the 1940s and the 1950s. Average NFL salaries have risen from $33,000 a year in 1974 to nearly half a million dollars in 1992.[26] But the vast majority of people who have capitalized on the Phase III economic environment are certain kinds of lawyers,† doctors,‡ and most of all, businessmen and -women. For every professional athlete earning over $200,000 per year, there are hundreds of these other kinds of people with equal incomes.

Increasingly, business people with high incomes are not the un-educated, self-made men who struck it rich in Phase I of U.S. big company capitalism. Nor are they the college dropouts who started high-tech businesses in their garages in the '50s, '60s, and

---

*The number of billionaires worldwide, as reported by *Fortune*, has more than doubled just in the five year period 1987–1993.

†Law has become so lucrative in a more competitive and less stable world that the number of lawyers operating in the United States grew from 343,000 in 1971 to almost one million in 1989.[27]

‡Medical doctors now earn nearly six times as much as the average person, with MD incomes going up twice as fast as average in the recent past.[28]

'70s. Globalization has added significant new levels of complexity to decisions, and those able to handle that complexity increasingly seem to be individuals with a good education, often from excellent schools.* They are people with degrees from Michigan or Stanford or Penn or MIT who provide leadership or do deals in a small consulting or financial services or real estate company. Compared to a professional football quarterback, they are invisible. But they often make exceptionally good money.† And unlike the sports star, they do so for four or five decades instead of just one.

One popular explanation of this new economic pattern centers around Ronald Reagan, but the argument does not fit the facts.‡ The growing range of income distribution started before Reagan. 1973 is the date when that and other new trends seem to begin.§ And there is evidence that these phenomena are not just found in America.‖ The pattern is global and has powerful implications for everyone.

*Labor economists have found that, in general, there has been a sharp rise in earnings for college graduates relative to high school graduates over the past fifteen years.[29] The average yearly wage for an individual in the United States without a high school diploma is $14,078. High school graduates make $19,567, college graduates make $32,728, and those with professional (graduate) degrees earn $65,648.[30]

†In 1993, the winner of the income sweepstakes appears to be George Soros, a Wall Street trader, who made $650 million.[31]

‡By popular, I refer to what is communicated by the mass media (newspapers, TV). The Reagan administration clearly took actions that fostered a Phase III economic environment, and thus all the good and bad that has come with that environment. But the administration did not create Phase III. The new economic era was underway well before Reagan took office.

§For example, aggregate gross income that went to the highest ½% of taxpayers fell for years until bottoming out in 1973.[32] Oil prices took off in 1973, going from three dollars a barrel to thirteen in 1986.[33] After decades in which the dollar was worth exactly 360 yen, the exchange rate started going down in 1971 and was only 130 by 1987.[34]

‖The increasing number of billionaires over the last two decades is clearly a global phenomenon. In just the past four years, the income range in the for-

---

In its totality, the post '73 economic shift is very complex. But at its core, the change is really quite simple.

Imagine, for a moment, a Thursday night poker game among a group of six friends. The same six individuals have been playing for a long time and the game has become as much a social event as a competition. To assure that no one loses or wins too much money, a number of formal and informal rules have evolved. Raises are limited to twenty-five cents and three per round. Only two or three relatively simple kinds of poker are allowed. If anyone starts to win too much, he usually eases up. If anyone begins to lose too much, others look for an opportunity to give that person a victory. The sophistication of play is not very high and there is no trend to make it better. But the arrangement is very comfortable for all involved.

Now introduce the following changes. Three newcomers are added one Thursday night, all whom have had very different poker "careers." The newcomers successfully goad the regulars into their kind of play: dealer's choice instead of just three kinds of games, no limits on raises, and no informal norms to restrict competition. Five hours later, the results are predictable. The quality and sophistication of play are higher than usual, as are both the opportunities and hazards presented to the participants. At 1:00 A.M., the distance between the biggest winner and the biggest loser is considerably larger than is normally the case. Also, the regular who normally wins the most is not on top because the skills needed to play only two kinds of poker and the skills needed to play a broader range of dealer's choice are different.

---

mer USSR and Eastern Europe appears to be growing explosively. According to the European Foundation of Entrepreneurship Research, the number of entrepreneurs in that region grew tenfold between December 1989 and April 1992. The most successful of these individuals have very sizable incomes.[35]

To a significant degree, the same kind of changes have been occurring in the economy and in the workplace. As a consequence of
globalization and other forces, new competitors have entered
many industries, markets have grown in size, and all kinds of rules
limiting competition have dissolved. Some of these rules were formal: government regulations, labor agreements, corporate bureaucratic policies. But many were informal, the "I won't hit you if you
won't hit me" variety or the "let's all set our prices at this level"
pattern that evolves in classic oligopolies. Fewer barriers to competition have usually increased the fighting, the instability, the
speed of change, the problems and opportunities for producers,
and the availability of higher-quality or lower-priced goods/ser-
vices to consumers. And just as in the hypothetical poker game,
both the strategies and career paths needed to win have also
changed in some very important ways. What worked well for
much of this century—especially large-scale bureaucracy and professional management—is less often leading to success. In the post
1973 economic environment, what looks unconventional to a mid-
20th century eye is often winning—for Jeremy King and many
other people like him.

---

### NEW RULE #2
The globalization of markets and competition is creating enormous change. The new rule is: to succeed, one must capitalize
on the opportunities available in the faster-moving and more
competitive business environment while avoiding the many
hazards inherent in such an environment.

# PART II

## NEW RESPONSES

# 4

# FOUNDING AND GROWING SMALL BUSINESSES

PEOPLE HAVE FOUND OPPORTUNITIES IN SMALL BUSINESSES AND entrepreneurship for centuries, but a Phase III economic environment has recently increased the attractiveness of those ventures. Part of this is due to the decreased attractiveness of many big established firms. Part is due to the comparative advantages that small firms have in a faster-moving business environment. Still another part is due to the increased ease of setting up a business in an era with facsimile machines, mobile phones, inexpensive photocopiers, and personal computers. But for whatever reason, find a dozen successful people today and you will probably be surprised at how many have found their opportunities in a small business.

---

Very few of those in the Class of '74 have worked only for small companies. Between 1964 and 1973, almost all were employed at least once in a medium-sized or large firm, if only for a summer job.[1] Even when they chose companies in 1974, 71% went to big corporations. But in 1992, that figure had shrunk to 38%. The rest, about 62%, were with small firms. Because there are fewer manufacturing companies among small corporations than among large, this shift in the class toward small business is directly related to the trend away from manufacturing.[2] A single statistic says it all. In 1992, the typical MBA from Harvard's Class of '74 worked for a firm that employed, in all its businesses and in all its locations worldwide, a total of 550 people. And that firm manufactured nothing.

To a large degree, this relentless movement away from big business is the natural result of mixing pyramidal organizations with ambitious and competitive people. Not everyone can move up, so aggressive non-movers have some incentive to try to become bigger fishes in smaller ponds. This applies to our 115 MBAs as well as to most people who have gotten into good educational programs: in business, law, medicine, architecture. To get into such programs, people usually need high standards and a strong drive to win. This is more true today than in 1974, and much more true than in 1949. In the 1940s, one in two applicants was admitted to Harvard Business School. In 1974, one in three got in. Today, the acceptance rate is one in six. People who successfully fight their way through all the hurdles needed to get into that kind of program do not sit comfortably in the middle of tall hierarchies.

This general problem was exacerbated for the Class of '74 by the very nature of many of the big businesses they encountered. These firms were not just big, they were also often very bureaucratic, centralized, and political.

A few statistics are helpful here. In 1955, 75 of the 100 largest revenue-producing industrial businesses in the world were clearly "American" organizations.[3] In 1992, the top 100 list had only thirty U.S. corporations.[4] In 1970, six of the ten largest banks in the world were U.S. based.[5] In 1992, none of the top ten were American. The largest U.S. bank ranked only 25th in the world.[6] In general, the last two decades have been tough on big U.S. businesses, especially compared to the 1940s, '50s, and '60s. Most obviously have not gone broke, and a few have done exceedingly well. But in a more competitive global business environment, many firms have discovered that they were overstaffed, too inward

looking, political, bureaucratic, somewhat arrogant, lacking sufficient leadership, and even experiencing diseconomies of scale. To
some degree, all such problems are the consequence of large size.
But these difficulties are also very much the result of years of success in much less competitive environments. As Jim Heskett and I
have documented at length in *Corporate Culture and Performance*,
being in a dominant position for too long can easily create organizational cultures that are lethargic, myopic, and risk-averse.[7] As
long as the competition is weak or oligopolistic, as it was for many
American businesses in a Phase II economy, big firms can succeed
despite these weaknesses because of their great strengths: vast financial and human resources, strong brand loyalty, thousands of
patents, and so on. Only when a Phase III economic era emerges
do the weaknesses begin to hurt significantly. Then, inward-look-
ing and bureaucratic corporate cultures not only reduce profitability and growth in the short term, they can also inhibit firms from
doing what is needed to make them into stronger competitors over
time.[8]

When Class of '74 MBAs first encountered big corporations in
summer jobs around 1965 or full-time jobs in 1968, many of them
did not like what they saw. Bureaucracy created severe limitations
on what they could do. Politics created internal labor markets and
promotion processes that sometimes looked to them much less like
meritocracies than like old boy's networks. Those who accepted
jobs in big firms in 1974 put up with these problems for a while.
But many eventually gave up and moved to smaller businesses.

When Lisa Martin left school in 1974, she went to work for IBM
in sales. When asked in 1992 about that experience, she was blunt:
"I absolutely hated it. In a sense, I was a square peg, and they only
had round holes. At one point when I was in training school, they
pulled me aside and said that if I did not straighten up, they would
send me home on a plane. They wanted me to change my attitude
toward rote memorization and sales pitches. 'Thank you, Mr. Customer, for giving me an opportunity to discuss with you the
IBM. . . .' In retrospect, I really admire IBM because they were
able to take many individuals and make them into very good sales-

people. But they did not necessarily know what to do with someone who could learn the whole manual in a couple of days. Now,
what do I do? I used to go to sleep. We were supposed to be learning the manuals and all the product features. That took a couple of
days. How long can it take? We were fresh out of school. We were
used to absorbing information like that. It wasn't just me; it was
everybody. We went and watched television all day. We didn't do
anything. They had allotted six weeks for us to learn two manuals,
and we were to spend six weeks doing it, even if it didn't take six
weeks. It was really frustrating for me because I can't stand not
having something to do." Not surprisingly, Lisa left and in 1977
founded her own company (see profile on next page). Despite
dozens of problems and headaches of the sort one often finds in
small business, she is still an entrepreneur in 1993.

Some will see in Lisa's comments an arrogance and self-
centeredness which they find unattractive. But in her generation,
especially among the well educated, most would view her attitude
with much sympathy and empathy.* IBM and firms like it feel too
much like their image of the Kremlin. Or even worse, many big
companies seem like the big government in Washington that created Vietnam and Watergate.

---

Pat Hayes actually tried to reform Kremlin-like firms.† Described
by classmates as clean-cut and somewhat idealistic, Hayes joined a

---

*The U.S. population in general is not enthralled with large firms these days.
In a 1988 Gallup poll, big business was ranked last in a group of ten in terms
of how much confidence people had in various institutions. But our group of
115 is even more critical than the average person and can offer more specific
reasons for their criticism.
†I think the Hayes story is particularly interesting because, if one had polled
the faculty in 1973 about the kind of graduate they were trying to produce,
Pat would have received very high scores.

# LISA MARTIN

## BUSINESS EXPERIENCE

### Quilts and Bedding Inc. (1977–1993)                    Albany, NY

President and Owner. Started this business venture in retail baby bedding. In 1980, bought out competitors and doubled the size of the business. In 1985, changed the direction of the company from retail to wholesale. In 1986, increased business volume three-fold. Doubled sales volume in 1987.

### Hinkel Jordon Stores                    Los Angeles, CA

Assistant Buyer. Planned and coordinated purchases of women's apparel for west coast stores.

### IBM                    New York

Sales Representative. Met with potential customers on both an appointment and cold-call basis. Solved customer problems. Prepared letters, proposals and sales presentations.

### Aldine Research                    Chicago, IL

Controller/Treasurer (1972). Responsible for short- and long-term planning, cost accounting, budget planning and review, and scheduling.

Office Manager (1971). Coordinated the efforts of the office staff, responsible for hiring and firing. Created office accounting system.

Secretary (1970). General office responsibilities.

## EDUCATION

### Harvard Business School                    Boston, MA

Received Masters of Business Administration degree, 1974.

### University of Illinois                    Urbana, IL

Received B.A. in Social Studies and Education, with distinction, 1970. Member of Urbana Tenants Union and Dormitory Council.

## PERSONAL

Born in 1948, raised in Illinois. Father a self-employed building contractor. Mother an interior designer. Oldest of four children.

Married in 1979 to Jack Guilford (a stock broker). Three children, ages 13, 10, and 6.

Quote: "It's so easy to fall into a pattern of doing what you should do instead of what you want to do. (1975)"

large manufacturing company after Harvard hoping to pursue a career of helping big corporations become more innovative. Today he is running a small non-manufacturing business.

Hayes was born near Columbus, Ohio in November 1946. When he was only one year old, his father received an MBA and then went on to pursue a Ph.D. in business administration. Mr. Hayes never finished his dissertation however and spent much of Pat's childhood moving from state to state seeking teaching jobs. The family's weak financial position was always a sore spot for Pat and led him to begin working at a very young age. Money was in particularly short supply during his high school years. "We were in a smaller house than ever before," he recalled, "and I remember having to do my homework in the bathroom, using the toilet for a seat and the laundry hamper as a desk." By his senior year, he was working thirty hours a week in a local Ben Franklin five and dime, and, as he remembers, "most of the money was passed on to my mother."

After Hayes graduated, both of his parents were offered teaching positions in Los Angeles. Due to financial constraints, Pat grudgingly followed them there to begin studies at UCLA. In addition to making the freshman crew and winning the PAC 8 championship (after having never played sports in high school), Pat underwent a philosophical shift spurred by the social movements that embroiled his college campus. "My traditional notions about grades and a degree began to fade away under fire of the 'now' values of living each day more fully, as opposed to gritting one's teeth. Dostoevsky and Camus were powerful influences." Pat's academic performance was poor during this period. "Grades were either A's or F's. I remember a course in which the final exam angered me in its simplistic 'repeat after me' approach, so I turned it in blank in protest. The professor gave me an incomplete which later lapsed into an F. If I liked the course, I did well; if it was not of interest, I procrastinated. I just didn't see any reason for going through the intellectual hoops necessary for a grade. The free speech (and later the anti-war) movement had caught my fancy and I joined the marches and rallies, tossing back tear gas canisters shot off by the police."

After many trials and tribulations, including taking a year off and being on academic probation, Hayes eventually graduated with a degree in economics (having earned a 3.9 G.P.A. in his last two years). Even today he says he never abandoned his earlier rebellion against going through school chasing after grades. "What happened is that I became interested in really getting a thorough understanding of the course material, and grades naturally fell into place."

After graduation, he worked for nearly three years in management positions with the federal government and a private natural resources firm. In the process, he developed a keen interest in line management. "It was only about a year prior to starting the HBS curriculum that I considered business school," he wrote in 1974. "Before, my options seemed to be either law, economics, political science, or diplomacy. What I kept finding from my experience was that I could easily pick up the functional skills necessary but that what had differentiated my performance was an ability to organize, to plan and coordinate, to appreciate the big picture or task, and integrate the different inputs. Business school was viewed as the best place to sharpen these management skills."

At HBS, he became fascinated with the required course in Production and Operations Management (POM) and subsequently took a summer job at a large manufacturing firm. He then focused his second year job search almost entirely on line jobs in large U.S. manufacturing companies. In April 1974, he accepted a position to work with a select team in a large corporation to open a new and innovative plant. The firm's CEO hoped this facility would solve what was then called "the blue collar blues" problem and thus improve the company's productivity and quality.[9]

Beginning in the summer of 1974, Hayes participated in the development of the new plant, helped hire the workforce, and started up the first production lines. But in correspondence from January 1975, he already was showing signs of disillusionment. "Too many people in the manufacturing organization are not interested in building a world class plant. They seem to be convinced their historical methods are just fine." Hayes tried to overwhelm the resistance with hard work. Seventy hour weeks were common. But by the spring of 1976, he realized that as difficult as life was in his innovative plant, working in the firm's more conventional manufacturing operations would be much worse. "After two successful years, it became clear that, aside from the unique, experimental environment in my plant, my next assignments would be in a setting where there was no interest in or enthusiasm for someone like myself. Because of good product design and service, the firm had never learned to be a world class manufacturer. And most people were uninterested in changing these realities. My hard work seemed to receive little recognition or support. The situation was demoralizing."

In February 1976, Hayes quit his job but did not abandon big business. Instead he joined an even larger manufacturing corporation. With much work and somewhat more political savvy, this time he prospered. Over a four year period, Pat took on increasing responsibility, eventually becoming the youngest manager of a large plant in the entire company. "We introduced new programs in labor relations, project management, contractor relations, cost control, minority hiring, and safety. Our use of computers was innovative in our industry. I also worked relentlessly to upgrade the capabilities of my management team." By 1981, he had hired sixteen additional MBAs and sent two managers through the Sloan program at Stanford.

During this same period, much like Jeremy King, Hayes got involved in a number of ventures outside of his company. He and a group of others bought a restaurant, a gas station, and some other real estate. Unlike King, Hayes never hinted in any of his correspondence that he was considering getting out of corporate life. To the contrary, in January 1981, he reported that he thought he had a chance of some day becoming the president of a large company.

1981 and 1982 were tough years for Hayes. Because of his successes, he continued to push the company in directions he felt were consistent with his CEO's emphasis on entrepreneurship inside the firm. But his initiatives led to a series of more and more difficult conflicts with a new and more conservative boss. He looked for support at corporate headquarters and found few people willing to get involved in the disputes. "Initiative after initiative was blocked. By November of '82, I felt the situation was intolerable." As a result, in December of that year he took a 20% pay cut and went to work for his state's governor in a major cabinet-level job.

Hayes remained in the public sector for nearly two years. He found that experience to be both exhilarating and productive, but eventually the politics made the work as frustrating as life in a big corporation. In late 1984, he accepted a job as president and CEO of a very small non-manufacturing business (see profile on next page). In 1994, Hayes was in a related job, as president and owner.

Over the past decade, Hayes has learned that life in a small and entrepreneurial venture is very different from a big organization and that the differences are not all for the better. Without massive financial and human resources, he has had to work very hard at times. "More than once it has seemed that the wolf was at the door ready to have us for lunch." Nevertheless, he has not seriously considered going back to big business, at least at this point in his life. He is happy where he is, and slowly, he is succeeding in a significant way. In 1993, he reported a net worth of $3 million.

On December 15, 1987, Pat Hayes wrote a letter to the editors at *Fortune* magazine in response to their November 9th cover story on Harvard Business School. He said he agreed with many of the observations made in the story: that Harvard MBAs are increasingly not pursuing executive careers in large manufacturing businesses and that this trend was disturbing. But he said he disagreed with their conclusions about causality. "In short, the environment and not the salaries can be the most discouraging aspect of pursuing a line management career in large industrial companies today. The politics and bureaucracy are stifling, especially to high-caliber and high-potential graduates of leading business schools. The

# PATRICK HAYES

1991–1993     P. Hayes Ventures, Portland, Oregon
- President and Owner

1984–1990     Timberwolf Real Estate, near Portland, Oregon
- Chairman and CEO

1983–1984     Oregon State Government
- Commissioner, Department of Transportation and Public Facilities

1976–1982     Radcliff Industrial Group, Michigan and Illinois
- Plant Manager (1980–1982)
- Senior Plant Engineer (1978–1980)
- Administrative Supervisor (1976–1978)

1974–1975     Michigan Engine Parts, Flint, Michigan
- First Line Supervisor in plant

1969–1972     California State Government, Forestry Department

EDUCATION

1972–1974     Harvard Business School—MBA

1965–1969     UCLA—B.S. in Economics

PERSONAL

Background: Born in 1946, raised in California, Texas, and Ohio. First of four children. Father a professor, mother a school teacher

Marital Status: Never married. One child, age 10.

Interests: Cross Country Skiing, Distance Running, Sky Diving, Hiking, Horseback Riding, and Stock Market Speculation

Quote: "I give the arrogant incompetent no recognition, and am unsympathetic to those who resign themselves to mediocrity. The man who strives gains my respect, even if it be for something antagonistic to my interests. (1974)"

word gets back quickly. When you have the option of beating your head against the wall in a poor environment versus going to Wall Street, BCG, or McKinsey, where they encourage, develop, protect, and clearly guide the talent, the salary differential is only the icing on the cake."

The environment Pat found in small firms was more to his liking. In this respect, his story is very common in the Class of '74.

---

Pat Hayes, Lisa Martin, and others have found in smaller firms more opportunities for broader, less bureaucratic, more influential, and hence more satisfying work (see Exhibit 4.1). In 1985, I asked all 115 of the MBAs a series of questions that psychologist Richard Hackman has found can differentiate jobs in terms of potential to be personally satisfying.[10] On average, they rated the po-

EXHIBIT 4.1

Overall Satisfaction with Work
In Small Versus Medium and Large Firms
For 115 Class of '74 MBAs

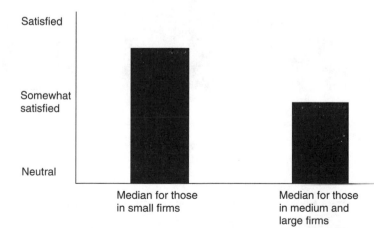

Based on 24 questions asked in 1990 and 1991.

sitions in smaller firms higher. Those jobs were reported to give people more feedback, more autonomy, more ability to see work through from start to finish, and more chances to use their own judgment.[11] Likewise, when asked about problems in their jobs, those in small firms reported fewer that tend to influence job satisfaction (see Exhibit 4.2). People in large firms were more likely to complain about having too little authority, too much ambiguity, too many conflicting demands, and too little influence.

Phil Cadel is typical. He worked for a dozen years at a large U.S. corporation and then switched into a smaller business. In a 1992 interview he described the situation this way: "The top management at my previous employer always said I could do anything

EXHIBIT 4.2

Problems Faced by the Class of '74
In Their Jobs in Large Firms Versus Small Firms*

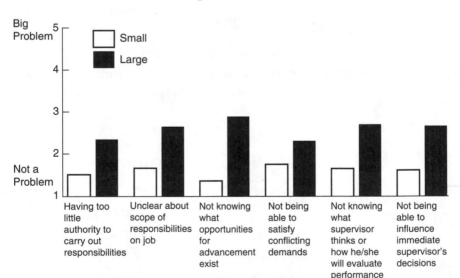

*Data based on self-reported answers to a 1984 questionnaire. All differences are statistically significant at .05 except "not being able to satisfy conflicting demands."

I wanted within my area of responsibility, but it just wasn't true. Here it really has been true. I feel that I've made a tremendous impact on this company. Everybody has; it's not just me. I've been able to use some theories that I always thought were true, but I was never able to test. The first year I was here, we lost money. We broke even the year after that. We made more money than people thought we could make in this business a year after that, and last year we made three times that much. I don't think it is always going to progress that way. In fact, this year we will probably go back to the level we were at two years ago, which was considered a good year. But that's a very adequate return on the investment, and I'm pleased and proud of what has happened.

"What is even more exciting is that our managers are finally at the point where they are enthusiastic about what they are doing and they feel that they have the authority and ability to make changes, and report on the results to us, instead of calling us up and asking what the solution to a particular problem is. They have been making improvements in productivity, in quality, and in personnel through training.

"It's really a fun place to work," Cadel says with an enthusiasm that is relatively unusual today. Yet his comments are not rare among the Class of '74. "I have never dreaded getting up and going to work, but I've never had the degree of satisfaction that I have here. I feel I've grown twenty or thirty times in the six years that I've been here, compared to the nearly twelve years before that."

In smaller firms, particularly in entrepreneurial situations, the MBAs also found much more upside income potential. In contrast to big businesses, economic possibilities were tied closer to the ability to get their firms to perform well. All this did not guarantee high incomes.* The difference was that the structure of opportunities in smaller firms, especially for entrepreneurs, was more like a real market. If customers loved their products or services, they could literally become rich in ways that were not possible in most big business.†

---

*The median 1991 income for the bottom quartile among entrepreneurs was $100,000. The median income for the top quartile was $800,000.
†Of those Class members with net worths above $5 million in 1992, 90% made their money in small businesses.

Entrepreneurs have always held a special place in the hearts of many Americans. Yet for every ten people who think about trying to be an entrepreneur, less than one actually acts on that idea and really succeeds. What can be learned from the Class of '74 about what is required to be an effective entrepreneur?

When I began teaching at Harvard in 1973, there was a theory about "windows of opportunity" for founding a business. The gist of this was that most HBS graduates who succeeded in starting something of their own did so in the time window between their fifth and tenth reunions. Before the fifth, they were not ready. They did not have the experience, the business idea, the financial backing, and so forth. After the tenth, they became too locked into a corporate way of life, too conservative, and too unwilling to risk what little wealth they had accumulated. Or so said the theory.

The top third of Exhibit 4.3 shows the actual timing statistics for the Class of '74. As is clearly evident, the window theory does not work for this group. Between their fifth and tenth reunions, less that 25% of the successful entrepreneurs started their businesses. Furthermore, there is no other five year window that nets over 50%. 1985–1989 has the single largest grouping at $47^1/_2$%. That period is also distinguished by a very robust economy.

When we think of entrepreneurs, the popular image is often Steven Jobs or Ken Olsen or Bill Gates—that is, people who invent products that are manufactured. Yet 90% of the Class of '74 entrepreneurs are outside of manufacturing. *Ninety percent.* They have gone where entry barriers are lower and where opportunities are more numerous.

Who are these people? Remarkably, on many many dimensions they are very similar to all the rest of their classmates, even those in big business. I have examined over 200 factors and found only a half dozen or so that seem to distinguish the entrepreneurs. In other words, on most dimensions, they are not a breed apart. But they do tend to be more independent than is typical for the class

and more hard working. They also have a greater need for autonomy and a lesser need for security.

Although I cannot prove this assertion, I suspect that the pattern
shown at the bottom of Exhibit 4.3 also differentiates the average
person in the class from the population at large. This could help
explain why so many in the class have become successful entrepreneurs.

### EXHIBIT 4.3

### Entrepreneurs in the Class of '74

*When to start a business?* The percentage of Class of '74 entrepreneurs who have founded businesses in each of the following years
is:

| 1975 | 1976 | 1977 | 1978 | 1979 | 1980 | 1981 | 1982 | 1983 |
|------|------|------|------|------|------|------|------|------|
| 0% | $9^1/_2$% | $2^1/_2$% | 0% | 8% | $2^1/_2$% | $9^1/_2$% | 0% | 5% |

| 1984 | 1985 | 1986 | 1987 | 1988 | 1989 | 1990 | 1991 |
|------|------|------|------|------|------|------|------|
| 8% | 14% | $9^1/_2$% | $9^1/_2$% | 5% | $9^1/_2$% | 0% | 8% |

*What kind of business?* For the Class of '74 entrepreneurs, the
biggest pattern is this:

| Manufacturing | Nonmanufacturing |
|:---:|:---:|
| 10% | 90% |

*Who should be an entrepreneur?* Within the Class of '74, entrepreneurs and nonentrepreneurs are more alike than they are different. The biggest exceptions are these:

|  | Entrepreneurs | Nonentrepreneurs |
|---|:---:|:---:|
| Independent* | 68% | 49% |
| Very Hardworking* | 80% | 34% |
| Need Autonomy[†] | 90% | 73% |
| Need Security[†] | 2% | 18% |

*Based on extensive psychological testing conducted in 1973
[†]Based on a 1983 questionnaire

An argument is sometimes heard that runs like this: talented people leave big firms, especially large manufacturing companies,
mostly to make more money. This drain of talent hurts big firms
and all the constituencies that depend on them. Often the people
most hurt are lower-level workers who lose their jobs and, unlike
Harvard MBAs, have great difficulty finding new ones at equal
pay. The whole situation is unfair.

Undoubtedly there is some truth in this argument, but how
much? Is it bad for the economy that most of Harvard's Class of
'74 are not working in large businesses? Is the rush to small business a symptom of greed? For at least three reasons, the best answer to these questions is clearly not a simple yes.*

---

*Two additional reasons offered by those in the Class of '74 are these. First,
given the tendency of large bureaucracies to be somewhat wasteful with
human resources, it is not guaranteed that MBAs would actually accomplish
more as full-time employees of big firms. A standard joke in many large companies is that no one listens to a middle manager until he or she quits, becomes a consultant, and then offers the exact same advice back to the former
employer at four times the price. Although obviously rather cynical, there is
some truth in this attempt at humor.

Second, it is not at all clear that inwardly focused organizations and highly
competitive people combine to produce useful outcomes. Many, if not
most, large businesses in the 1970s and '80s were inward looking. (What
is amazing today is that most people did not even realize this tendency until Peters and Waterman wrote about it in 1982.)[12] When those kinds of
firms hire individuals like those in the Class of '74, competitive instincts
can easily turn inward, creating political problems inside companies and
giving the individuals reputations for being too career oriented or aggressive.
In more externally focused smaller businesses, those same instincts
can lead to behavior aimed at satisfying customers in order to beat competitors.

First, an examination of compensation and job titles for our 115 MBAs suggests that money may be less of a factor drawing some people to small business than is real responsibility and authority (see Exhibit 4.4). On average, those in small organizations do earn more, but not much.[13] The big difference comes in job title. Nearly three times as many people in small businesses have titles signifying positions of real power.

Second, statistics show that most managers in big firms do not create more new jobs today than do small business people. To the contrary, most managers in large organizations are shrinking em-

EXHIBIT 4.4

Income and Title Differences Between
Class of '74 MBAs in Small Businesses and
Those in Medium or Large Businesses

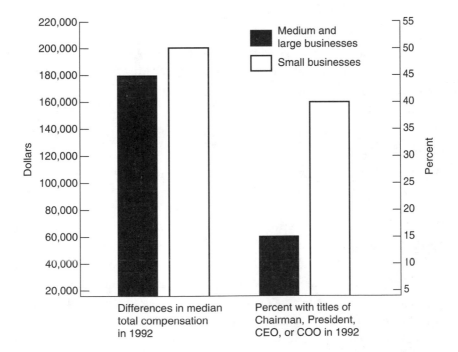

ployment* while small business people account for all new job growth.† Furthermore, recent studies have shown that these jobs created by small businesses are not just poorly paid service positions.‡ Small firms also produce much more innovation per employee or dollar than large firms.§ Of course, it is theoretically possible that Pat Hayes and people like him could save more good jobs or create more innovations as executives in big firms. This does happen. But it obviously does not happen very often.

Finally, although most of the Class of '74 are not working in big firms, most are involved in one way or another with efforts to help large businesses become more competitive. They do so not as employees but as consultants, suppliers, distributors, and financiers. The small firms led by Jeremy King, Pat Hayes, and Kevin Johnson all provide services to businesses, including big companies. Indeed, despite surface appearances, these MBAs have not abandoned big business. What most of them have abandoned is tall hierarchies, the organizational form used by big corporations for most of this century. That form is rapidly disappearing because it does not work well in a Phase III competitive environment. Tall command and control hierarchies are being replaced by a more flexible network form of organization. And as we see next, the Class of '74 and many other successful individuals are very much involved in the makeover.

---

*Incredibly, over $2\frac{1}{2}$ million jobs disappeared at Fortune 500 companies between 1973 and 1991.[14]

†Even as I write this in the summer of 1993, the prediction for the next two years is that all job growth will come from firms with less than 1,000 employees.[15]

‡David Birch says that between 1987 and 1992, while big firms killed 2,236,000 jobs with wages over $28,033/year, small firms created 2,296,000 of those higher paying jobs.[16]

§My colleague Jeffry Timmons has assembled data that show that small companies create two and one-half times more innovations per employee than large firms, two times as many innovations per R&D dollar, and two times as many innovations per scientist.

## NEW RULE #3

Increasingly, success is going to the small and entrepreneurial, not the big and bureaucratic. The new rule is: people who found and grow small organizations are often receiving both more job satisfaction and more income than most of those in traditional large organizations.

# 5

## CONSULTING TO AND ASSISTING BIG BUSINESS

THEIR RÉSUMÉS SEEM TO SAY THAT THEY HAVE ABANDONED BIG BUSIness, especially large manufacturing companies. Yet an examination of their actual work shows something quite different. The vast majority of Class of '74 small business people are very much involved with big business. But instead of acting as employees, they are suppliers, distributors, bankers, landlords, and consultants. And most of them think they add more value working on the outside rather than on the inside.

Everywhere today, big firms are being restructured so that they can better compete. This change has many aspects, one of which involves the replacement of tall bureaucratic hierarchies with smaller chains of command that are more loosely connected inside a firm and that are more tightly linked to suppliers or distributors outside the firm. Often called a network organizational struc-

ture,* this new form can be much more flexible, dynamic, innovative, and thus competitive.[2] Sometimes this restructuring occurs
entirely inside a large firm; a huge hierarchy is broken up into
smaller business units, the corporate staff is disbursed to the units,
a limited group at headquarters oversees the new company, and
all kinds of bureaucratic policies are thrown out or rewritten. For
a variety of reasons, more often this happens with outside help and
with the newly restructured organization partly outside the firm's
official boundaries.

Class of '74 member Harry Holtzman described a typical example of this kind of change in a 1992 interview. "The firm did well in
the first half of this century because of a visionary entrepreneur,
good products, the large and growing U.S. market, and probably a
little luck. After World War II, the company expanded and made
so much money that it developed a corporate culture that was
pretty stodgy and complacent. In 1976, growth slowed because of
increasing international competition. Management found a thou-
sand excuses why the slower revenue and profit increases were
not their fault, were not really so bad, and so on. In 1981, one en-
terprising division manager attempted to restructure his business
in a big way to make it more competitive. He apparently ran into
many obstacles: corporate staff, unions, his own managers, his
own boss. His failure led to a demotion and his exit from the firm.
This whole episode seems to have had a chilling affect on other
managers. By 1984, the financial results were so bad that a rumor
circulated that a small merchant banking firm was going to make
an unsolicited bid to buy the company. Management reacted by
selling one of its money-losing operations with help from a
medium-sized investment bank, and by hiring consultants from
two small firms. That's how I got involved.

---

*New forms are given many names. Handy, for example, talks about sham-
rock and federal organizations.[1] All share a number of things in common: 1)
they are less centralized, 2) hierarchies are shorter and smaller, 3) they are
more externally focused, 4) relationships across firm boundaries are sometimes stronger or more important than intrafirm relationships.

"My firm and one other group of consultants recommended many changes, the implementation of which required expertise the corporation did not possess. Five or six more advisory firms were hired. As a part of major staff reductions, a considerable amount of work was outsourced to give the company lower fixed costs. For example: a corporate audio/visual department was cut from around fifty employees to five and two outside A/V vendors were hired. For the same reason, the firm stopped manufacturing hundreds of parts and created a new supplier network. Even some of its sales force was cut, replaced by new arrangements created with distributors. To keep staff to a minimum, a few of the outside consulting firms and investment banks were asked to continue to work with the company over time as regular suppliers of ideas." These firms help sell businesses and buy new ones. They help reengineer outdated processes.* One MBA from these suppliers even accepted a full-time position as a vice president at the corporation.

"As you can imagine, the entire process was traumatic for nearly everyone. The uncertainties associated with potential job losses, with difficult strategic choices, and with all sorts of power struggles were very stressful. With the benefit of hindsight, it seems we got to where we are today via a most circuitous route. But where we are today [in 1992] is a vast improvement over a decade ago. The corporation is very different now. It is leaner, flatter, and less bureaucratic. Because some linkages inside the company have been loosened while others outside the corporation have been strengthened, the firm is more externally focused. Quality, productivity, and profits are up." Critics point out that employment is down significantly, as are some wages and benefits. The latter is true, the former is not. Employment *inside* the firm is down significantly. But employment outside the corporation has increased. The company is no longer a huge and rigid pyramidal

---

*Increasingly, the process of change from tall hierarchies to more flexible networks is being done under the conceptual umbrella of "reengineering."[3] During the 1980s, much of the work was done under the banner of "quality."

organization (see Exhibit 5.1). It is now more a coalition of smaller and flatter units both inside and outside the official firm boundaries (see Exhibit 5.2). Looked at this way, total employment may actually have increased.

EXHIBIT 5.1

Tall Hierarchies

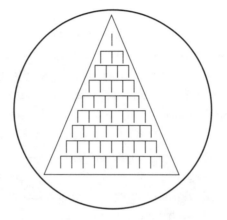

We have all been taught for so long to think of businesses as tall and stiff hierarchies of full-time employees that it is difficult to comprehend what is happening nowadays.[4] Some writers are arguing that hierarchies will disappear altogether, but that is highly unlikely. Instead, pyramids will continue to exist, because they can execute repetitive tasks very efficiently.* But in a more competitive and faster-moving world, hierarchies will become shorter, smaller, and less rigid. They will be connected with contracts and various kinds of shared understandings. Conventional notions about the location of a company's boundaries will also continue to have less

---

*Social science research extending back into the 1930s has consistently found that hierarchy can be very efficient under certain circumstances. In particular, hierarchy seems to work well with more routine and more repetitive tasks and less well with new or novel situations.

EXHIBIT 5.2

Flexible Networks

relevance.* All this is driven by the need to be more flexible, cost-competitive, and innovative in a Phase III economic era.[6]

Thus far, this change has been frightening for many people. They see tall hierarchies disappearing, and with them, a comfortable way of life. What they often do not see is that flexible networks offer huge, stimulating, and lucrative possibilities, especially for entrepreneurs, leaders, financial deal makers, and consultants.

---

*The extreme version of this idea, often associated with GE CEO Jack Welch, is of the "boundaryless corporation," where information and people flow easily between functions, divisions, nations, and even firms.[5]

No trend in the employment of MBAs from prestigious schools has received more discussion, or more criticism, than the movement toward consulting. As late as 1977, only about 15% of the Harvard graduating class chose jobs in that industry. By 1990, this figure had risen to 26%.[7] Since entry level consulting salaries have been 15 to 20% higher than other job offers, critics have said these statistics demonstrate a worrisome tendency on the part of MBAs to avoid tough but important jobs in favor of easy money. Although virtually no one has defended this trend, some have argued that an early consulting career is not so bad because it helps pay off educational debts and eventually sends graduates to high-level and full-time positions in large client firms. Although there is some truth in these arguments, they both miss a great deal. In particular, this way of thinking ignores the important relationship between the trend to consulting and the shift from hierarchies to networks.

Employment in consulting for the Class of '74 has not decreased over time. It has expanded slightly. In the spring of 1974, about $8\frac{1}{2}\%$ of our group accepted these jobs. In 1992, 10% of them worked in consulting. Money is undoubtedly important to these people, but it does not seem to be the central reason why many have chosen that line of work. Although those who accepted consulting jobs immediately after HBS commanded a premium over their peers' salaries, in 1992 the consultants actually made slightly less than their classmates.*

So why are one in ten in consulting today? Partially this is because that field is seen as offering a way to get executive positions in firms without having to work oneself up bureaucratic and politi-

*Consulting salaries in 1992 are pulled down, to some degree, by those who use self-employed consulting as a temporary assignment when they are unemployed or between regular jobs.

cal hierarchies. Partially this is because consulting is seen as a useful springboard to entrepreneurial ventures. The Class of '93 at HBS offers some validation to both these points. When asked at graduation what they expected to be doing in ten years, less than one in five of those who had accepted consulting jobs said "consulting."[8]

But the popularity of this industry is also very much related to the nature of the jobs themselves. Consultants from the Class of '74 do not work in large and bureaucratic organizations. Many are self-employed and thus have no bosses. Their assignments have a significant intellectual component, which is attractive to well-educated people. The job can be very challenging, which helps people to grow. And the focus of the work is often exciting because it seems important. Most of these consultants, most of the time, are not dealing with small or insignificant issues. Instead, they are being asked to help organizations survive and prosper by becoming more competitive. And more often than not, their clients are large corporations.

Consultants from the Class of '74 have been asked to help big manufacturing firms analyze where they are making and losing money. Consultants have been contracted to identify where firms have special strengths and where they are weak. Consultants have analyzed competitors, new market opportunities, acquisition candidates, and strategic plans. Consultants have been asked to help companies rethink marketing, manufacturing, R&D, finance, and personnel policies. Consultants have worked with employees inside corporations to reengineer work processes, to cut layers out of the hierarchy, to create more autonomous and market-focused business units, to change corporate cultures, and much more.

The demand for this kind of work has grown rapidly in the last twenty years and appears to be directly related to increased global competitive pressures. In a Phase III economic era, those pressures have exploded and, in the process, created a huge need for change inside businesses, especially large ones. That need for change, much of which can be characterized as moving from tall hierarchies to flexible networks, has led to enormous growth in the management consulting industry.*

Most of the assignments done by consultants could be undertaken by a firm's regular employees. Indeed, consultants often work as if they were special internal staff groups. Corporations use outsiders, often in a network-like manner, for at least four different reasons. Outsiders are usually more objective and less caught in the myopia of strong corporate cultures. They can literally see things that elude equally talented insiders. Outsiders can also more easily be the bearers of bad news than can full-time employees. The consequences of being fired as a consultant versus as a full-time employee are vastly different. Outsiders can specialize in certain kinds of problems in ways that are economically impossible for insiders, unless there is a huge corporate staff. Not even the largest of firms can afford a huge staff anymore. Moreover, the kind of people who are good consultants usually do not like working as full-time employees in big organizations. Efforts by large companies to build elite internal consulting groups have usually ended in failure.†

It is impossible to judge the effectiveness of all this consulting activity. Critics of the industry point out that although U.S. firms use many more consultants than the Japanese, the latter seem to have been winning. Some confirmation of this line of thinking can be found inside most large U.S. companies, where stories circulate of consultants earning big fees yet seemingly producing very little. Nevertheless, as the Class of '74 consultants are quick to point out, they sell their services one contract at a time or even one day at a time. Bad performance is punished by a lack of repeat business and by a shrinking reputation. If they were doing bad work, they say, the market would pay them poorly or eliminate them altogether. It has not; ergo, the criticisms are mostly unfair. For peo-

---

*The consulting industry has grown from about $1 billion in total North American consulting revenues in 1970 to $14.5 billion in 1991.[9]

†I personally have seen a dozen such attempts. Only one was successful.

ple who really believe in markets, the consultants' argument is convincing. But the controversy continues because not everyone really believes in the efficacy of markets.

Although there are critics, consultants also have many supporters. These individuals buy their services and occasionally make the consultants full-time job offers. In this manner, MBAs become executives in big business without having been promoted up tall, bureaucratic, and political hierarchies. For some headstrong individuals, bypassing the internal promotion process is probably the only way they would get an executive position in a large company today.

---

Clyde Galvin has spent most of his post MBA years at a well-known consulting firm. Born in 1950, Galvin was raised in Arizona and attended college at Yale before coming to Harvard. He performed well in graduate school and established a reputation among his classmates as being cerebral, articulate, and analytically sophisticated. "I think he got the best grades of any of us," says one of his peers with clear admiration. Another classmate is less flattering: "The professors loved him. Personally, I got tired of listening to him pontificate."

Upon graduation, Galvin was obliged to take a two year assignment in Washington. He then joined the Boston Consulting Group when they were still a small and young company (see profile on the next page). Over the past two decades, Galvin has worked on over a hundred assignments, some lasting for years. He has also helped BCG grow in size and reputation, manage the transition from founder CEO to the second generation, and develop new ideas and tools.

In a 1992 interview, Galvin talked about the excitement, especially during his first decade in consulting, of trying to help the top management of large companies deal with major issues. "There have been some pieces of work that have been very intellectually challenging. I like the feeling of working in a close fashion with

# CLYDE GALVIN

BUSINESS EXPERIENCE

Boston Consulting Group                                    Boston, MA
- Vice President and Practice Area Leader (1990–1993)
- Vice President (1982–1990)
- Manager (1979–1982)
- Senior Consultant (1978)
- Consultant (1976–1977)

Department of Defense,                                    Washington, D.C.
Office of the Assistant Secretary
- Lieutenant and Research Analyst

EDUCATION

Harvard Business School                                    Boston, MA
- MBA with distinction, 1974

Yale University                                            New Haven, CT
- B.S. in Physics

PERSONAL

Background: Born in 1950, raised in Minneapolis and Chicago. First of four children. Father was manager in a large advertising agency, mother was not employed outside the home.

Marital Status: Separated. Two children, ages 12 and 10.

Quote: "Back in 1975 before I went into consulting, I was pretty sure I didn't want to work in a big bureaucracy. I had had a couple years of that and I knew what that was about. I was reasonably sure that most corporate jobs, and even a lot of so-called professional jobs like being a banker, had to do with being part of a big bureaucracy, with all the meaningless stuff and bowing and scraping and inertia that was involved with that. (1983)"

some very good minds on tough problems. I really enjoy tremendously team interaction and coming up with solutions that go far beyond people's expectations." In a number of cases, Galvin has been on multiple projects with the same company and thus gotten to know the senior management well. "In one instance, I worked with a firm for ten years. I feel as if I have had significant impact on the company. That has been very satisfying. In another case, I am absolutely convinced the client would not be in business if it were not for the massive changes that my colleagues helped top management to make. That company today has fewer full-time employees, a different business mix, a much more external orientation, and significantly better productivity. Being a part of that has also been extremely satisfying."

Galvin makes much more money today than the average person in his class (around a half million dollars a year). He also admits, somewhat reluctantly, that work at a well-known consulting firm is not all glamour and big bucks. Classmate Peter Pfeifer is much more explicit. "When I left a big manufacturer after ten years to join a major consulting company, I didn't really know what to expect. It has turned out very well, but it was gut wrenching at the time. I frequently had an uncomfortable feeling in my stomach as I sought out clients or initiated consulting projects. Even today, now that I'm well established, I often feel that my career is like that of a professional baseball player. As long as my batting average is high, I will continue to be successful. But if my average declines, I may quickly end up in the minor leagues. Of course, this is a fair market environment, but it is also pretty Darwinian and requires a lot of effort and focus to maintain success. During my first decade in business, as a manager in a big company, I had a reasonably balanced life. Over the past decade, I have had less and less time to do anything except work. Sometimes I feel I will only get a chance to rest when I retire. This is not what I expected when I left school."

Trevor James has also felt overworked as a consultant, although less so today than a decade ago. James started with a consulting firm immediately after graduate school. Then in the early 1980s, he encountered a frustrating series of conflicts with his boss. "He played a lot of games with people. When he was traveling, he would call someone up early in the day. He would tell them that he was going to call back at six o'clock. That was a mechanism to make sure you were still there at six o'clock. Then of course he wouldn't call until six thirty. It was like a joke, but it wasn't that funny." In 1982, James quit and set up his own private practice. He specializes in one industry where, today, he is relatively well known. His assignments focus mostly on important strategic choices that firms are being forced to make in an increasingly fast-moving business environment (see profile in Chapter 3). As his own boss, James has also had more control over his schedule and has therefore been able to be more responsive to his family. This feature of self-employment seems to be attractive to many people these days.

---

When Anthony Decolina left Harvard, he also went to work for a consulting firm. Two years later, he accepted a job offer from one of his clients, a small temporary help business. Decolina started as the firm's executive vice president and general manager. He eventually became the president, CEO, and part owner. The move from a very prestigious to a very unprestigious industry has worked out exceptionally well for Anthony.

The temporary help business has boomed in the past twenty years. Between 1982 and 1990, temporary employment in the United States grew ten times faster than overall employment.[10] The growth is directly related to the shift from tall hierarchies to flexible networks. In a more competitive world, U.S. businesses have been forced to reduce their fixed costs. One way firms have done this is by staffing for minimum demand when possible and using temporary help to fill in peak periods. Costs are then reduced, hierarchies are made smaller, and the firm's boundaries become less clear. Anthony's organization has been a successful provider of those temporary services. As a result, Decolina has made even more money than the consultants in his class.

John Nully has done something similar, only his "temporary" employees are highly skilled lawyers. Over the past two decades legal departments in many large businesses have been cut and their work farmed out to law firms that specialize in business services. Nully has greatly benefited from this trend. Some of these same corporations have also been outsourcing work associated with employee benefits, corporate travel, product design, accounting, and data processing.[11]

When Garrett Morgan left Harvard, he was employed for six and one-half years in a large U.S. manufacturing company. After six jobs in three different countries, he quit big business in 1980 and launched his own firm to distribute overseas certain types of U.S. TV programming (see profile on the next page). In an increasingly global economy, the market for U.S.-produced programming is growing. Morgan's small firm helps link creators in the United States with customers outside America. In contrasting his tenure as an employee in a big firm versus his time as a small supplier and distributor to large organizations, Morgan says: "My corporate activities all seem like useless bureaucracy today. Budgeting, controlling, management meetings, and so forth. I don't have the feeling I ever contributed to building something of durable value. My own firm is now ten years old, and has served many thousands of customers with a unique product. There is pride in this."

About 5% of Garrett's classmates are also acting as distributors, mostly for large businesses. They help route chemicals, steel, TVs, appliances, jewelry, and other items from producer to consumer. In most cases, they work very closely with producers, almost acting as small divisions of larger firms. In some cases, the services they offer were once actually performed by the producers themselves. Today, the larger firms rely on outside distributors either to reach new global markets or to offer more specialized services to their customers. The arrangement is very much in the spirit of flexible network organizations.

# GARRETT MORGAN

PROFESSIONAL

| | |
|---|---|
| 1981–1993 | International T.V. Programming Inc., London |

• Founder and owner

| | |
|---|---|
| 1974–1980 | Bartok Manufacturing Industries, New York, Atlanta, Brazil, London |

• Director of Finance for Europe, Plastics Division (1979–1980)
• Special Assignment in Brazil (1978)
• Assistant to the President (1977)
• Manager of Financial Operations (1976)
•  Manager of Product Planning (1975)
• Financial Analyst in the Packaging Division (1974)

| | |
|---|---|
| 1972–1974 | Harvard Business School |

| | |
|---|---|
| 1970–1972 | New York University |

• B.A. in Business and Public Administration

| | |
|---|---|
| 1968–1970 | Brooklyn Community College—A.A.S. |

PERSONAL

Background: Born in 1946, raised in Germany and New York. Youngest of three children. Father was a violinist, mother was a pianist.

Marital Status: Married in 1990 (second marriage) to Helen Bork. Three children, ages 17, 10, and 4.

Briefly describe an ideal scenario for you ten years from now: "If I stay in corporate life, I'll own a nice home in Connecticut, I'll have a child or two, I'll earn $60,000 (today's purchasing power), and I'll be close to V.P. If I run my own business, I'll work like a dog, have millions in the bank, will have divorced two wives, and look age 65. If that doesn't sound ideal, that's why I'm still working the corporate life. (1979)"

When Kyle Robbins finished school, he went to work for Hewlett Packard. Since 1983, he has been employed by small high-tech companies that invent, make, and sell equipment exclusively to large semiconductor manufacturers. These corporations rely on small suppliers because the latter are often more creative and faster moving. In this way, Robbins is still highly involved in big business, only now his base is a firm with only 120 employees.

In 1974, Martha Pennings joined a commercial bank where she became a banking officer serving large and medium-sized corporations. In 1979, she moved to a small investment banking company, and then in 1981, she helped found her own firm. The job and company changes were very challenging at times, but they helped her grow and obtain the type of employment she desired. Today, Pennings works closely with companies to raise money, evaluate acquisition candidates, and buy or sell businesses. Like a number of her colleagues in investment banking, she too is helping restructure corporations so that they can better compete in a Phase III economic era. But she does so as a member of a company that has less than twenty employees (see profile on next page).

Phil Cronin joined a medium-sized real estate development firm when he left graduate school. In 1980, he went to a similar but smaller firm. Today, he provides office space to businesses of all sizes in a large metropolitan area. There was a time when some of his tenants would have owned their offices. Today, they do not want to tie up scarce assets in real estate, so they lease space. Two or three percent of Cronin's classmates are doing something similar in other metropolitan areas.

This same kind of story repeats itself again and again in the Class of '74. They may work officially for small firms, but they are very much involved with big business. Their résumés say that they have abandoned large organizations, especially large manufacturing firms, but in reality they have not. They serve those organizations as consultants, distributors, financiers, landlords, and in still more ways. In a Phase III economic environment, they often earn considerably more by operating on the outside instead of on the inside. And most of them are absolutely convinced that they are also

# MARTHA PENNINGS

WORK EXPERIENCE

Hodskin, Pennings, & Co.(investment bank)          Stamford, CT
  • Co-founder and President (1981–1993)

Walters Securities                                 Greenwich, CT
  • Junior Partner and Managing
    Director (1979–1981)

Bank of Massachusetts                               Boston, MA
  • Vice President (1978)
  • Commercial Banking Officer (1977)
  • Assistant Loan Officer (1976–1977)
  • Management Trainee (1974–1975)

EDUCATION

Harvard Business School                             Boston, MA
  • Masters in Business Administration, 1974

Wellesley College                                  Wellesley, MA
  • A.B. in Applied Math and Biology, 1969

PERSONAL

Background: Born in 1947, raised in Minnesota, and Paris. Second of six children. Father (Belgian) was a professor of chemical engineering, mother worked as a bacteriologist until she married.

Marital Status: Married in 1971 to Richard Pennings (runs his own engineering business). Two children, ages 18 and 11.

Why did you leave The Bank of Massachusetts?: "I basically wanted to be independent and self-supporting. I wanted to make my own course. I also got to the point at the Bank of Massachusetts that I had learned a lot, and I was learning less and less as time went on. I saw an opportunity, and so I made the switch. (1983)"

much more useful working from the outside. A typical comment: "Over the past decade, I think I have helped one well-known large manufacturing company a great deal. The managers inside the firm say so. But I cannot imagine being an executive there. The constraints and politics would drive me crazy and render me relatively ineffective. As an outsider, I have been able to do things and say things like no insider—not even the CEO. Maybe some day this will change; working there now is, I'm sure, much better than a decade ago. But the firm still has a way to go."

They have not abandoned big business, but they have left something behind—tall command and control hierarchies, with the usual emphasis on conformity. The Class of '74, and especially the most successful members of the class, deal less with vertical relationships that link them to a relatively homogeneous group of people and more in horizontal relations to a more diverse crowd. In this sense, they offer a preview of the future for many people: a future with less hierarchy and management, but more market-like relations, diversity of players, negotiation among individuals, and a greater need for leadership.

---

NEW RULE #4

Huge and inwardly focused hierarchies perform poorly in fast-moving and competitive environments. As a result, big organizations everywhere are being forced to slim down, become less bureaucratic, and form closer relationships with customers and suppliers. This trend offers great opportunities—for small distributors, suppliers, and especially business consultants.

# 6

# PROVIDING LEADERSHIP

ALTHOUGH MANAGEMENT WAS THE CENTRAL TASK NECESSARY TO make tall hierarchies function, in flexible networks that process is less important, especially relative to leadership and negotiation/deal making. Leadership is necessary to create, grow, change, or shut down the smaller and more volatile units found in networks. Deal making is necessary to help structure transactions and other relationships between these units. Executives must still usually know how to manage, but without leadership and some negotiating skills their career advancement is increasingly being limited. This very important change has not gone unnoticed by most of those in Harvard's Class of '74 or by other successful people like them.

---

In 1987 and 1988, I interviewed the ten top executives in each of twenty businesses, firms that had all been very economically successful over the previous five to ten years.[1] Among the questions I asked were these two: 1) Think of someone you know who you feel has done an outstanding job of managing whatever he or she was responsible for and then describe in as much detail as possible what this person has been doing that adds up to outstanding management. 2) Think of someone you know personally who, in your opinion, has done an absolutely outstanding job of providing effective leadership to the people and activities around him or her, and describe again in as much detail as possible what the person has been doing that adds up to outstanding leadership. I took the resulting 200 stories about great management and great leadership from this very credible group of interviewees and looked for commonalities. As you might expect, a lot of what was recorded was idiosyncratic to a particular time, place, and person. But there were some recurring themes in both the management stories and the leadership stories, and the two were very different.

Outstanding managers were described as people who were very disciplined at planning and budgeting. They took time to plot what actions, taken by whom, at what cost, would achieve various goals. They were also said to be very systematic about maintaining organizations that could accomplish those plans. They selected good people, trained them, put the right person in the right job, communicated plans, and delegated. And they were described as skillful at monitoring organizational results versus plans, spotting deviations, and quickly getting activities back on track. As a result of these actions, outstanding managers were unusually successful at making organizations function the way they were designed to function—producing certain products or services, at the right quality, on time, and on budget.

Outstanding leaders were described as people who made sure an organization had clear and sensible direction, usually by helping to create a vision of the future and strategies for achieving that vision. Leaders were said to communicate that direction widely and in such a way as to get relevant parties to both understand it and believe it is appropriate. Great leaders were also described as being unusually good at motivating or inspiring people so that when progress toward a vision encountered serious problems there was enough energy to break through the barriers. In doing all this, leaders were said to produce change—developing new organizations or businesses and helping old ones to adapt to a shifting business environment (see Exhibit 6.1).[2]

In the relative stability of a Phase II economic era, many firms performed very well with managers and executives spending much more time managing than leading.[3] With demand equal to or greater than supply in many industries, the key to success was simply getting the product out the door on time and on budget. In a more competitive and changing Phase III environment, this is no longer true. In some industries, supply exceeds demand. In others, what is being bought is constantly changing. In both cases, it is no longer effective to do well only what has been done in the past. To succeed, organizations now need to reduce costs, improve quality, develop new products, and move much faster. The capacity to produce useful change is becoming more and more the key to success. And change requires leadership.

Those organizations that have been most successful in coping with the post '73 economic environment often have moved from tall hierarchies to structures that look more like flexible networks.* As a part of that change, they have delegated management functions to lower-levels and asked middle to upper executives to spend much more time providing leadership.[4] The idea that only a few people in a firm should try to lead is slowly dying.

In this new economic environment and in network-like organizational forms, executives who cannot lead are increasingly having problems. If they are surrounded by other non-leaders, their firms usually perform poorly unless protected in some way.[5] If they are surrounded by leaders, people who cannot lead are increasingly being passed over for promotion. This pattern can be

---

*For example, this aptly describes what has happened over the past decade to GE, the most successful of the giant U.S. manufacturing firms.

## EXHIBIT 6.1

### Management and Leadership

| | Management | Leadership |
|---|---|---|
| Creating an agenda | Planning and Budgeting—establishing detailed steps and timetables for achieving needed results, and then allocating the resources necessary to make that happen | Establishing Direction—developing a vision of the future, often the distant future, and strategies for producing the changes needed to achieve that vision |
| Developing a human network for achieving the agenda | Organizing and Staffing—establishing some structure for accomplishing plan requirements, staffing that structure with individuals, delegating responsibility and authority for carrying out the plan, providing policies and procedures to help guide people, and creating methods or systems to monitor implementation | Aligning People—communicating the direction by words and deeds to all those whose cooperation may be needed so as to influence the creation of teams and coalitions that understand the vision and strategies, and accept their validity |
| Execution | Controlling and Problem Solving—monitoring results vs. plan in some detail, identifying deviations, and then planning and organizing to solve these problems | Motivating and Inspiring—energizing people to overcome major political, bureaucratic, and resource barriers to change by satisfying very basic, but often unfulfilled, human needs |
| Outcomes | Produces a degree of predictability and order, and has the potential of consistently producing key results expected by various stakeholders (e.g., for customers, always being on time; for stockholders, being on budget) | Produces change, often to a dramatic degree, and has the potential of producing extremely useful change (e.g., new products that customers want, new approaches to labor relations that help make a firm more competitive) |

*Source: A Force for Change: How Management Differs From Leadership*, by John P. Kotter (New York: Free Press, 1990).

easily seen within Harvard's Class of '74. Those individuals who manage but do not lead are in lower-level positions, are making less money, and are in slower-growing businesses than their classmates.*

---

Sammy Ludorff is not a naturally charismatic person, although he has a certain charm. Overweight and with a wardrobe that defies fashion, he has been more successful than most of his classmates at providing businesses with leadership over the past twenty years. This ability became especially visible after a job change in 1982. At that time, Ludorff joined a company called Kalmachet Industries. The firm had total sales of $250 million, divided into three divisions. Sammy's job was to head the smallest of the three, basically four facilities with 1981 revenues of about $40 million and 300 employees. He accepted a base salary that was 10% lower than at his previous employer, but negotiated several bonus and stock option plans that offered lucrative possibilities if the division's performance could be significantly improved.

Ludorff spent much of his time during his first three months at Kalmachet talking first to his managers, then to other employees, then customers, and finally suppliers. He used these meetings to build rapport, to listen to peoples' ideas about the business, and to assess the individuals with whom he would be working. After these many discussions, he took his top ten managers to a banquet room at a local hotel and talked with them for two days about the future. "I summarized what I had learned from my one-on-one meetings. Then I said I wanted to work with them to develop a clearer sense of where we wanted to take the business, and how we were going

---

*Class of '74 members who are acting as managers today seem to be doing so for two reasons. Some are in companies with cultures that simply do not allow people to lead. Others seem to want to lead, but are blocked by something inside themselves.

to get there. The discussion was slow at first, which is only natural. They were all still a little wary of me, the overeducated outsider. But by the end of the two days, we were beginning to get at some real issues."

The "futures" meetings continued, on and off, for months. As Ludorff's credibility grew, he became more aggressive in raising questions and challenging assumptions. When the management began to gather and analyze different kinds of information, they reached some surprising conclusions. Although they had always thought of themselves as manufacturers, over 50% of revenues were coming from after-sales service and other non-manufacturing aspects of the business. Although they had always considered Awkwright Industrials as their key competitor, they found that most competition was coming from a company that was not even in their industry a dozen years before.

More than a year of meetings was required to produce even the beginnings of a vision. During that time, Ludorff replaced only one of his managers ("The poor man should never have been put in that job"). He also spent a great deal of energy making sure short-term results were good so as to bolster his standing with his corporate bosses.

In September 1983, seventeen months after he arrived, Ludorff orchestrated a day-long meeting for nearly 100 people, including all of his management and staff, key individuals from the corporate office, two board members, a dozen executives from important suppliers and customers, and the mayor of the local community. The session was a combination of information sharing and hoopla. Dressed in a way that endeared him to his factory workers and left yuppie managers slightly embarrassed, Sammy told the audience about the "futures" discussions. Others talked about the conclusions that had been drawn thus far and the emerging business strategies. What the presentations lacked in slickness was more than made up for by the enthusiasm of the speakers.

During 1984, the pace of change increased considerably. Groups within the division were reorganized, one facility was rebuilt, task forces worked on dozens of subjects, and twice the normal number of new products and services were introduced. A few of the initiatives ran into major problems, but successes outnumbered failures by a goodly amount. Ludorff's role during this period varied between being chief cheerleader and chief fireman. "There were a few times when I feared that the problems created by change might actually overwhelm us," he reported later, "but somehow we prevailed."

In September 1984, almost one year to the day after the launch meeting, a second event was held, this time for nearly 200 people. "It was incredible," Ludorff reported in an interview later that same year. "I had nearly half of my employees there, including some of the senior people who weren't in managerial positions, some of whom I'm sure had never been to a meeting like that in their entire lives. We celebrated our successes for the past year and talked about the future, about how we wanted to become one of the leading companies in our business in the entire world. Some of the managers had adapted an old Springsteen song for the occasion. Everyone got a good laugh out if it, but it also really charged people up. The day ended with beer and a great barbecue. It was a real happening."

When the pace began to slow down somewhat in 1985, Ludorff promoted two change agents to key positions and brought in a senior executive from the outside. Each of the three initiated more activities, all operating under the umbrella of an increasingly clear division-wide vision. In August 1985, when one of the facilities won a major award from an industry association, Ludorff suspended work one day at 3:00 P.M. for all 335 employees and held a celebration.

An assessment of the overall results by 1986, four years after Sammy's arrival, looks something like this. Revenues were up 100% to nearly $80 million. Net income had increased by over 200%. Employment had grown from 300 to 340. Productivity was up over 50%. The number of new services and products introduced yearly had also doubled.

Reflecting back on this in 1992, Ludorff said: "The biggest change, at least in my opinion, was less in the economics than in people's attitudes and in the culture. This had not been a bad company, and it wasn't in trouble in 1982, but it wasn't going anywhere either, and it wasn't going anywhere because nearly everyone was too content with the status quo. They didn't have a sense of either the problems or the opportunities on the horizon. They had neither the hopes nor the fears that you need to really perform well today. By 1986, the organization was very different in that regard. And that began to pay off big in terms of economic results."

---

Harvard Business School mythology would have us believe that most graduates, by their 20th reunion, would be providing their organizations with effective leadership. The extensive criticism leveled at MBA programs in the last decade would suggest that few, if any, of these people really lead. An obviously interesting question is: Where lies the truth? Is Sammy Ludorff the rare exception? Or is he the norm?

By looking at their jobs, their own yearly descriptions of what they do, and the nature of their accomplishments, I would estimate that between 40% and 50% of the Class of '74 are acting primarily as leaders and are doing so with at least a moderate degree of effectiveness.* None will challenge Winston Churchill for space in the encyclopedias. But at least 10% of them, representing 4% to 5% of the overall group, deserve a grade of excellent. Sammy Lu-

---

*This estimate is based on the yearly information they have supplied about their activities and on their responses in 1992 to a question about their biggest business accomplishment. Individuals were designated leaders if they talked about creating and communicating a vision, gaining commitment to the vision, and inspiring people to high levels of performance, and if there was real evidence that they had produced meaningful changes in a group of people.

dorff is in that group. Another 20% to 40% might be graded very good. Even the remaining 50% to 70% do, in a modest way, what all great leaders do: create direction, obtain commitment, and inspire action.

Class of '74 members in large organizations who supply leadership usually do so to renew their lethargic businesses, a task that is rarely easy to accomplish. Ralph Orteges has worked since 1987 for a large Spanish manufacturing company (see profile on next page). His assignments have been almost exclusively focused on trying to turn around, sell, or shut down parts of his company to help make the firm more competitive. Jim Gibbs helps run the Far East operations of a large well-known U.S. manufacturing corporation. Over the past five years, he has hired a new staff and refocused the company on customer service, quality, and growth. After much work, he thinks his organization is now widely perceived as the best of its kind in his part of the world. Heinz Hoffman started his post HBS career in consulting and then moved into banking. Over the past four years, he has been helping to redirect a German bank with a new strategy and structure, many fewer managers, and a smaller branch network. According to Hoffman, it has been a tough four years.

Hoffman, Gibbs, Orteges, and a number of their classmates are all providing leadership to help firms look less like the tall hierarchies shown in Exhibit 5.1 and more like flexible networks displayed in Exhibit 5.2. They do this by cutting layers out of the management hierarchy, by creating more autonomous and customer-focused units, by forming closer relationships with suppliers and distributors, by selling businesses, by reducing staff levels, and sometimes by buying new businesses. Typically, all this is done with enormous difficulty due to unadaptive corporate cultures, political resistance to change, time and resource constraints, and just plain uncertainty over the best course of action. Some people feel the compensation does not really make up for the pain and hours worked, but the money is not shabby. Hoffman, Gibbs, and Orteges averaged nearly $400,000 in income in 1992.

Others in that class who provide leadership in large organiza-

# RALPH ORTEGES

PROFESSIONAL

1987–1993    Ibarra Electronics                    Madrid, Spain
- Group Vice President (1990–1992)
- Division General Manager (1989)
- Head of Ibarra USA, New York (1987–1988)

1980–1986    Seville Pharmaceuticals              Madrid, Spain
- Senior Vice President (1983–1986)
- Group Manager (1980–1983)

1976–1979    Clemson Chemicals        Lausane, Switzerland
- Manager of Market Development (1978–1979)
- Manager for Financial Planning (1977)
- Financial Analyst (1976)

1974–1975    Spanish Armed Forces
- Second Lieutenant
- Air Force Officer's Training Course

EDUCATION

1972–1974    Harvard Business School

1968–1972    Polytecnico de Madrid,
             Dr. of Engineering Electronics

PERSONAL

Background: Born in Madrid, 1945. Oldest of two children. Father was an accountant and personnel director for a textile company. Mother had a secondary school degree in teacher's training.

Marital Status: Married in 1978 to Carmen Iglesias. One child, age 9.

What have been some of the challenges, issues and problems you have had to deal with since HBS?: "From a strictly professional point of view, I think the problem is that you come out with great expectations. You are trained to be a general, though you may not have the personal qualities of a general. At best, you start off with a little lower rank as a lieutenant. You have to try to adapt to that. You have to try to become a general without offending people too much. (1983)"

tions are less concerned with radically restructuring their firms and more involved in making a flexible network form work well. Phil Bottinger has been employed by a highly respected electronics firm since graduation. His recent assignments have involved either creating or building small units within the company. In 1988 and 1989, he helped develop a state-of-the-art manufacturing organization, going from startup to 200 employees over a twenty-four month period. In 1990, he became the general manager of a fifty person business unit that specialized in tailoring certain kinds of equipment for a very specific market. Bottinger and people like him in big companies are trying to help these firms compete by behaving as if they were small businesspeople or entrepreneurs.

Class of '74 members who provide leadership in small organizations do so usually either to found or to build those companies. Barry Forman has created no less than four firms since he left business school (see profile on next page). When Francis Teller helped found an investment bank in 1979, it started with five employees. Today, it employs over fifty people.

The central leadership challenge faced by those in large and small businesses tends to differ somewhat. People like Hoffman, Gibbs, and Orteges often have to deal with corporate cultures in big companies that resist change and that crush leadership. Coping with those cultures can be a phenomenally difficult task.[6] Business founders like Francis Teller have to deal with the challenge of creating something from nothing despite very limited resources. In a small business setting, a few big mistakes can result in bankruptcy.

Class of '74 members who supply effective leadership sometimes conform to the images, usually from TV and Hollywood, that we often associate with leaders. Craig Rathborne actually is tall, handsome, charming, and articulate. But like Sammy Ludorff, most of these MBAs are less charismatic. They provide leadership not by interpersonal sparkle but by turning a relatively deep understanding of some business into a vision, by working very hard to get relevant people to believe in that vision, and by using their own beliefs and convictions to inspire others to action. It may not be highly photogenic, but it most certainly is leadership.

# BARRY FORMAN

BUSINESS EXPERIENCE

Wilco Consulting (oil field/financial services)               San Diego
* President, founder, and owner (1991–1993)

The Jamestown Consulting Group (environmental/medical consulting)
* Executive Vice President (1990)

Serundo Corporation (oil drilling equipment)               San Diego
* President and owner (1987–1989)

Forman Corporation (oil drilling equipment)               Phoenix
* President and owner (1985–1986)

Forman Construction (oil drilling equipment)               Phoenix
* President and owner (1976–1984)

The Walker Group (automotive industry consultants)               Dallas
* Assistant to President (1974–1975)

Procter & Gamble               Geneva
* Marketing Assistant, international marketing group (1971–1972)

EDUCATION

Harvard Business School, Boston, Massachusetts. MBA, 1974.
University of St. Gallen, Switzerland. M.A. in Economics, 1971

PERSONAL

Background:  Born in 1945, raised in Switzerland.  Youngest of two children.  Father was CEO of one of Switzerland's largest companies, mother was not employed outside the home.

Marital Status:  Married (second marriage) in 1986 to Caroline Sloane (in medical school).  One child, age 15.

Give a candid evaluation of your strengths and weaknesses: "On the whole I am optimistic and do not lack confidence.  These characteristics plus the fact that I am very ambitious combine to make me a rather strong-willed person.  My drive and ambition tend to make me impatient toward myself and others.  In trying to reach a goal I sometimes become self-centered and overlook the feelings and needs of other human beings. (1972)"

An interesting question: What differentiates Rathborne, Ludorff, Forman and other leaders from the rest of their classmates? Clearly they behave in some ways that are different (see Exhibit 6.1). But what about the underlying psychology? And what about their career paths?

Given all that has been written about leadership, one might expect to find hundreds of personal or career dimensions on which leaders are different, since they are seen to be a "breed apart." Nevertheless, of the nearly 500 factors on which I have quantified information, those who provide leadership are clearly different on less than a dozen (see Exhibit 6.2).

The leaders in the class are more oriented to power, recognition, prestige, and growth than are their peers. They are also less oriented toward security and leisure time. In terms of career paths, the leaders are a little less mobile, moving through fewer companies and industries. They are also more likely to have had a general management career and to be employed in a large business.

What I find most interesting about Exhibit 6.2 is all that is not there. When I began analyzing the information on the class in 1990, I fully expected to find that the leaders would be a recognizable subgroup on many personality, background, and career dimensions. This has not proven to be the case. The implications are most intriguing, especially regarding how many people can reasonably expect to be able to grow into effective leaders.

Another interesting question: where did Sammy Ludorff and others in his class learn to be leaders? What role did Harvard Business School play? What about parents and early life experiences? How much was learned after graduate school?

In a narrow sense, the best answer to the question about where

EXHIBIT 6.2

Leaders

|  | Class of '74 Leaders | All Others in the Class |
|---|---|---|
| *Who Are They?* | | |
| What Is Important in a Job?* | | |
| Personal Growth | Higher | |
| Professional Growth | Higher | |
| Power | Higher | |
| Recognition | Higher | |
| Prestige | Higher | |
| Current Income | No Difference | |
| Future Income | No Difference | |
| Intrinsic Nature of Work | No Difference | |
| Autonomy | No Difference | |
| Security | | Higher |
| Leisure Time Available | | Higher |

*Asked in 1985

|  | Class of '74 Leaders | All Others in the Class |
|---|---|---|
| *Career Paths* | | |
| Number of Industries '74–'92 | 2.2 | 2.7 |
| Number of Companies '74–'92 | 2.6 | 3.3 |
| Movement Into Mostly General Management Jobs | 60% | 19% |
| Mostly Big Employers | 42% | 26% |

they learned to lead is: on the job. The actions they are taking in 1994 that constitute leadership would not have been possible in 1974. Back then, they did not have the industry-specific knowledge, the reputation and relationships, the deep appreciation of what constitutes good leadership, nor some of the interpersonal skills that they have and use today. They picked up these additional assets on the job, by watching others and through trial and error.[7] And much was learned in small business settings because big corporations often had neither sufficient role models nor an environment which would allow the kind of experimentation needed to learn effective leadership.[8]

In a broader sense, the answer to the learning question is: in their pre-HBS years. The basic elements upon which leadership grows were in place for most of them before puberty. These factors include internal drive (since producing change is hard work), some minimum level of intelligence (because vision in complex business environments requires good thinking), a lack of heavy neurotic baggage (which interferes with information gathering and relationships), and integrity (the lack of which repels people).[9] Some combination of genes, prenatal care, nutrition, parents, and schooling created these building blocks.

The MBA program's role in developing this leadership potential with a curriculum, at least in a direct sense, was very limited. There was no "Leadership" course.[10] There were no explicit attempts to develop leadership skills. Used in class, the term "leadership" had many and vague meanings, including what today we would call management or administration.

But in other ways, Harvard probably did play a role of some importance, starting with the admissions process. Unlike many schools, grades and test scores were not the dominant factors in selection decisions.* A variety of less quantitative indices, many of them relating to leadership potential, were used to assess candi-

---

*In the mid-1980s, Harvard became the only business school in the United States not to require the Graduate Management Admissions Test.

dates for the Class of '74. The admissions office gathered information on applicants' extracurricular activities while in school and on their job experiences. They asked people to write long answers to essay questions and then read those responses for clues about maturity, integrity, and self-insight. They interviewed candidates when possible and required references from bosses and teachers. The process was time consuming, expensive, and vulnerable to much criticism* But key players at the School were convinced it produced many more students with leadership potential than a system that relied mostly on grades and test scores.

Harvard took these people, after they arrived in Boston, and tried to make them even more ambitious and more self-confident that they could fulfill their ambitions. With a very challenging program, it also demonstrated that if they went into tough situations, requiring hard work and producing stress, they could grow a great deal. The combination of leadership potential, a drive to compete, a willingness to learn, and a Phase III environment then pushed these people to try hard to develop needed leadership skills on the job so that they could succeed. These factors influenced class members to look for good role models and to move away from companies that would not give them demanding jobs where leadership could be learned. As a result, over an extended period of time, many developed some capacity to lead. The very same kind of process probably helped them to learn to be entrepreneurs and small businesspeople. (I will have more to say about this in Chapter 9.)

Would more of them be leading today or be leading more effectively if Harvard had focused explicitly on leadership (or entrepreneurship) in the curriculum? I think the answer is yes, although I can offer little in the way of proof. Certainly, they could have been taught more about this in their two year stay in Boston. But even more importantly, with no explicit emphasis on leadership in their courses, I fear that too many of them missed opportunities during

---

*The most common criticism is that the process allows for all kinds of biases to creep into the decision making.

their first five to ten years after school to grow their own natural capabilities. Too many had to figure out, by themselves, what leadership was, why it was important to individuals other than CEOs of large firms, and how leadership skills can be developed on the job. Surely this process could have been accelerated with some alterations in the curriculum. The same is probably true for entrepreneurship.

Today, anyone choosing a business program is well advised to look carefully at how schools deal with the question of leadership.

---

NEW RULE #5

Success in managerial jobs increasingly requires leadership, not just good management. Even at lower levels in firms, the inability to lead is hurting both corporate performance and individual careers. Organizations that stifle leadership from employees are no longer winning.

---

# 7

## DOING DEALS

STAN ROBERTS LIKES TO COMPETE. AT ONE POINT THIRTY YEARS AGO, he hoped for a career in the National Hockey League. Sports stardom has never materialized, but today Stan is rich and influential—as a managing director of an important investment banking firm (see profile on the next page).

Born in 1951, Roberts grew up near Montreal, the second of three children. His father was an engineering manager who worked in a small company owned by Stan's uncle. Roberts usually did well as a student. Some of his teachers believed his spirited disposition was the only factor that at times prevented him from achieving top marks. At age twelve, he entered the same small Canadian boarding school that his father and uncles had attended and then almost got expelled on the first night after getting into a fistfight with one of his new classmates. Young Roberts claimed the boy put pool cue chalk on his pants. His classmates say that Stan was just trying to establish "who was who."

Roberts was occasionally in trouble throughout his four years at boarding school, but the way he tells it, those years represented some of the best of his life. He made many lifelong friends and was awakened by a new level of academic and athletic rivalry that he

# STANLEY A. ROBERTS

PROFESSIONAL

| | | |
|---|---|---|
| 1974–1993 | The Blackburn Investment Bank | Tokyo, Japan |

- Managing Director and Head of Far East Finance. Managed all of Blackburn's Asian Investment Banking Coverage Officers (1987–1993).
- Managing Director and Partner. Responsible for Japanese business development (1985–1987).
- Principal. Responsible for equity and private placement business in Japan. Undertook first interest rate swap at Blackburn with best client, generating $1mm in revenues (1983–1989).
- Vice President. Managed Tokyo office (1980–1983).
- Senior Associate. Opened Tokyo office with 20 other people (1978–1983).
- Associate. Worked on large energy related project in London, Tokyo, and New York (1974–1977).

| | | |
|---|---|---|
| 1972–1974 | Harvard Business School | Boston, MA |

- MBA, second year honors.

| | | |
|---|---|---|
| 1968–1972 | Harvard College | Cambridge, MA |

- B.S. in Electrical Engineering, magna cum laude. Varsity hockey.

PERSONAL

Background: Born in 1951, raised near Montreal. Second of three children. Father was an engineering manager in a family business, mother was not employed outside the home.

Marital Status: Married in 1978 to Gloria Able (an associate at Blackburn until the birth of their first child). Four children, ages 4, 6, 9, and 10.

Interests: Squash, reading, hockey.

Quote: "I think I've learned how to get people to move along and when to push someone and when not to push someone. That's a judgment. Sometimes in our business you've got to push a guy to do what you think is right. He's going to have a million reasons why you can't do it. That's a hard judgment when you're talking about a pretty big operation. You're really putting your judgment on the line and you live or die by it. (1983)"

found exhilarating. From the football field to academic contests to the all-important hockey rink, Roberts grew into a very successful competitor.  He was even selected to be a student prefect during his last year, a position which he says "gave me more responsibility and a free hand to modify some of the rules and restrictions which got me into so much trouble during my first two years."

The transition from boarding school to college was tumultuous: "Having never gone any farther than Montreal before in my life, traveling to Boston was a real experience. The first two months were horrible. I knew no one and was virtually awed by the physical plant as well as the people. Things got much better, though. Through hockey, I met a lot of people and found to my surprise that they were just as lost as I was. Sophomore year I decided to become a professional hockey player. I all but gave up working at school and passed only by a hair thanks to the school strike [in protest of the war in Vietnam]. Junior and senior years were different. The scare of almost failing combined with a hockey coach who was far from encouraging led me to decide hockey as a career would have to be postponed. Seeing I was financing almost all my own education through a scholarship and summer job money, I decided I better bear down and learn something."

Stan's determination led him to graduate with good grades and a degree in electrical engineering. He then sought admission to the business schools at Stanford and Harvard, a goal upon which he had been focused since his junior year. His aim was to attain the analytical tools, the personal connections, and the stamp of approval that he believed would allow him to become a business leader in the uppermost levels of management. His acceptance to these schools, like his selection as a boarding school prefect, represented a great achievement to Stan as well as something of a vindication: "One reason for coming to HBS was the attitude of some of my undergraduate friends. As an engineer, I had very few classes with most of them. This fact, combined with playing hockey and overindulging in some of the social aspects of undergraduate life, led some of them to see me as a jock type. This upset me to no end. So, when answering the question 'What are you going to do next year?' I took great pleasure in replying that I was going to attend the Harvard Business School. From those who didn't know me or had this jock image sewn up in their minds, the response was, 'God, I didn't know you were that smart.' My responding smile represented my sense of satisfaction of telling these egomaniacs that they could take their convenient stereotypes and . . .'."

Enrolling at HBS in the fall of 1972, Roberts enjoyed business school and performed well academically. His HBS experience reinforced his belief that doing better than his peers was central to his fulfillment. In 1973, he wrote, "If I can't evaluate myself against my peers, there will be no feeling of achievement, no goals, no satisfaction." He took a summer job with an investment banking firm and discovered that the industry met many of his needs. He accepted a position with a larger and more prestigious firm in that same industry after he graduated and then (somehow) talked his employer into giving him a nine month leave of absence to do a low budget world tour. In Asia, he earned his way teaching English. In Latin America, he worked as a cook and common laborer. In Australia, he sold second-hand cars. It was, to say the least, quite an adventure, and one which played a formative role in his career development. "The Business School gets you so geared for jobs and career; people kept saying, 'What are you doing this for?' Well, in my eyes, it set the pattern that I was going to do the things that I thought were right for me. Nine times out of ten you are going to run into situations where, by not doing the obvious or the standard, you benefit at some point in time."

During his first three years in investment banking, Stan worked in New York, Tokyo, and London. The experience was hectic, but very educational. Because he was critical of the way the firm's small Far East operation was run, he was given the opportunity in 1978 to be part of a team sent to Tokyo to build that business. He accepted despite warnings from many of his peers that the firm would eventually close the Tokyo office because previous efforts to make it grow had failed.

Roberts began work in the Far East with a group of fifteen people. Away from New York with its traditional beliefs about how to do business and in a difficult business climate, they tried new approaches to what Stan described in a 1981 interview as the firm's core business: "Developing vehicles that bring together, from around the world, people who have capital and people who need capital." In the more global and more unstable Phase III economic environment, increasing numbers of people have wanted capital to grow or turn around businesses, and increasing numbers of people have been able to provide that capital. Stan has flourished in this deal-making environment. "The only real problem was that I was often lonely. But the business was a great challenge and great fun. We developed a wide variety of ideas, many of which the people in New York thought were slightly crazy. But most worked." His loneliness faded as he met his future wife at the firm and as he developed close relationships with a number of his clients. Those client relationships, in turn, helped generate more business for his group.

In 1980, he was promoted to Vice President; in 1983, to Principal. During this time, the Far East operation grew substantially. In 1982, Stan assumed responsibility for Australia/New Zealand and began generating significant fee income. In 1985, he became a Managing Director and Partner. In this role, he helped both manage and lead his organization, but his biggest activities were still associated with providing financial services and deal making.

When interviewed in 1983, Stan was working very long hours. "I've decided that there's a certain period in my life when I'm going to work exceptionally hard so as to create sufficient net worth to cover any future need. Then I want to spend a lot of time with my children and give them what I had, which was a fantastic childhood. This may be a pipe dream, but I think we all need those kinds of aspirations, especially when you are still working at 3:00 in the morning."

Although he has only a small ownership interest in his firm, Roberts has already been able to accumulate a significant net worth. In a globally competitive economic era where many corporations are created, restructured, expanded, bought, and sold, and where change is the norm, conservative and highly regulated commercial banks have often struggled. But many U.S. investment banks, willing to pay top dollar for talented people and to take calculated risks, have done very well. As of 1994, Stan is married and has four children. He still has a pretty good slapshot and his family's wealth is over $20 million.

––––––––––––

Financially oriented deal makers existed in large numbers in the 1930s, 1940s, 1950s, and 1960s, but not nearly as many as we see today and not nearly as well paid.* Back then, in a slower-moving, more regulated, and more nationally focused business environment, there were simply fewer needs and opportunities for these kinds of people. Globalization has changed this.

Increasingly, as businesses in Milan or Osaka have sought funds to expand into other parts of the world, they have found money in London and New York. Dealers play a crucial role in matching suppliers and users of capital. The volatility caused by floating exchange rates and increased competition has led to a substantial rise in the need for financial transactions. Such transactions are generally handled by dealers. In an age when many businesses needed to restructure in order to compete, mergers and acquisitions have boomed.† M and A is big business for financial dealers. Globalization has increased the sheer number of firms that might want to have relationships of some sort with other companies, especially those in other countries. Dealers often structure these relationships. The replacement of state ownership with capitalism in the former Soviet block and elsewhere, another consequence of

––––––––––––

*Statistics are hard to find, but total employment in the more visible investment banking firms, for example, was at least 500% higher in 1993 than in 1963.
†Between 1980 and 1989, in the United States there were close to 25,000 mergers or acquisitions.[1]

global competition, has created a huge movement toward privatization and restructuring. All this is usually handled by dealers.

Only a minority of the financial dealers in the Class of '74 work for the major investment banking houses. Nevertheless, almost all engage in one or more of the activities undertaken by these firms, such as trading, money management, mergers and acquisitions, leveraged buyouts (LBOs), and corporate finance. Often they act like any banker, helping to supply a firm with money. But they also act much like consultants, assisting the movement away from tall hierarchies toward flexible networks by helping sell off parts of companies. Sometimes they work very closely with firms in a flexible network style, acting almost like internal corporate finance or strategic planning staffs. Unlike consultants, financial dealers can also operate relatively independently of other businesses, investing in them through stock or bond markets. Sometimes their relationships with firms are even adversarial, as when they try to force companies to merge or be acquired.

Just as leaders try to create motivating visions and managers tend to excel at working in a formal hierarchy, dealers are usually market focused and excellent negotiators. While consultants are project oriented and entrepreneurs focus on their firms, dealers often look at the world in terms of transactions. They live and die to create transactions that can help businesses grow, start, turn around, or operate more efficiently. And because these transactions often involve a great deal of money, if dealers receive only a small percentage as a fee, they can become very wealthy.

In 1993, about 25% of the Harvard Class of '74 are mostly financial deal makers.* Even more are in financial functions or finan-

---

*All deal makers do more than just make deals. Stan Roberts has spent a lot of time providing leadership in his firm. But 25% of the Class appears to have jobs where the number one task is deal making. The remaining 75% can be placed into three categories: leaders (45%), managers (20%), and other (10%, including various kinds of individual contributors and those who have retired).

cial industries, but these others are not acting primarily as dealers; usually they are providing leadership to build businesses or turn firms around. On average, the deal makers make more money than do their classmates. In 1991, a typical income for a dealer was nearly $280,000 per year. Incomes for the remaining 75% of the class were about $160,000.* These high incomes, along with a number of other factors, make the dealers controversial, certainly much more so than leaders.

Of course, leaders are not always loved either. When they restructure businesses and in the process cut jobs, they can become the objects of fear and anger. But good leaders often seem very concerned about their followers. That behavior can make people respect them. Financial dealers are sometimes aggressive and self-confident to the point where they appear to be arrogant and uncaring. Sometimes they seem to be concerned only with making money. And to some people, they often appear to make money totally out of proportion to their contributions.

Given a choice between dealers and leaders as dinner companions, I think most people would choose the latter. But in situations where there are multiple players involved with different and probably conflicting interests, most people would probably want a good dealer on their side—even if he or she appears very aggressive and arrogant.

———————————

Troy Paxon may be the prototype of a dealer's dealer. He would probably have difficulty winning a popularity contest in most parts of the world today. Some of his classmates remember him as somewhat self-absorbed and instrumental in his relations with others. Nevertheless, he is exceptionally talented at one activity: making money.

Throughout his early years, Paxon lived in New York City, the

———————————

*Income figures are medians.

first of two children born to a couple that owned and ran a small retail business in Brooklyn. While in high school, Troy also worked in the family firm. The summer before starting at New York University he talked his way into a job in London with a U.S.-based trading company. At N.Y.U., he started a small business selling goods to fellow students, sometimes making over $300 a day. When he graduated in 1972, he came directly to Harvard Business School.

In the summer between his two years in Boston, Troy worked for the same trading firm that had employed him after high school. During the spring of 1974, he interviewed with four investment banking companies and six real estate firms and received only one offer, an outcome he now attributes to his youthful naïveté and lack of polish. He accepted that job and, in June, started work in a large real estate investment group as an assistant to the President.

In 1975, Troy began a sales job in his new firm. In 1976, he switched employers, taking a similar position at a smaller real estate company. His income fluctuated greatly depending upon sales commissions, but in general it was extraordinarily high for a man still not thirty years old. In 1978, he made over $200,000. When asked what he liked about his job, he replied: "Nothing, except the thrill of closing a deal."

In 1980, Paxon founded a trading and money management company. He used his own capital plus additional money from one other investor. In 1982, when his father's business ran into difficulty, he purchased that small company and for four years ran two businesses. In each case, he constantly, relentlessly, looked for new opportunities. In both businesses, he succeeded in finding them.

In the family business, Troy capitalized on the legalization of gambling in Atlantic City, New Jersey, increased the firm's revenues by nearly 400% over a four year period, and then sold the company for a good price. In his own firm, he developed new concepts for both trading and investing and created new systems that very successfully used emerging computer technology. The combination of a keen mind, hard work, intensive focus, and an increas-

# TROY PAXON

PROFESSIONAL

| | | |
|---|---|---|
| 1980–1993 | The Balderidge Group | Newark, NJ |

- Founder, Managing General Partner, and President

| | | |
|---|---|---|
| 1982–1986 | FRW Advertising Inc. | Newark, NJ |

- President and Owner

| | | |
|---|---|---|
| 1976–1980 | Jones & Langer Real Estate | Trenton, NJ |

- Vice President (1980)
- Salesperson (1976–1980)

| | | |
|---|---|---|
| 1974–1975 | The Wagner Real Estate Group | Baltimore, MD |

- Salesperson (1975)
- Assistant to the President (1974)

EDUCATION

| | | |
|---|---|---|
| 1972–1974 | Harvard Business School | Boston, MA |

Masters in Business Administration

| | | |
|---|---|---|
| 1968–1972 | New York University | New York, NY |

B.S. in Economics

PERSONAL

Background: Born in 1946, raised in New York City. First of two children. Parents ran a small retail business in Brooklyn.

Marital Status: Married in 1986 to Leah Coplon (not employed outside the home). No children.

Interests: Investing and trading.

Quote: "I'm no brain. I was nowhere near one of the brightest students at Harvard. As far as I'm concerned, there was no question that I was at the bottom of my class. But that hasn't stopped me. I just found something I like to do and I've done it really, really well."

ing number of interesting trading and investment opportunities all interacted well together. Troy began hiring additional help in 1981. By 1992, nine people worked for him (see profile on previous page).

When interviewed in 1991 in his relatively small and unpretentious office suite, Paxon was making nearly $2 million per year. He was recently married and had no children. In discussing his success, Troy said: "The key is: I don't give a damn what people think. I am willing to take risks, to do potentially stupid things, and embarrass myself. Most people won't do that. I recently called Jim Robinson [the then-CEO of American Express] and told him what a jerk he was because of the way he was handling the American Express card. It took me an hour to get through to him. I told him he was ruining a fabulous franchise. Others have drawn the same conclusion, but I had the guts to call him up."

Unlike many of his classmates, Paxon does not look back at Harvard Business School with much nostalgia. He feels the School taught him little that has been useful in his career thus far. He also resents the arrogance so often displayed by the School and its graduates. But Paxon does not appear to have suffered much as a result of Harvard. He has what some people would consider to be an exceptionally good life. He is his own boss and to a large degree controls his own destiny. He faces no bureaucratic or political barriers inside his firm. For the most part, he does what he likes to do. For this, he is compensated generously. If Troy keeps increasing his net worth over the next eighteen years at anything close to the rate of the past eighteen, he will be an extraordinarily wealthy man.

———————

The public's mixed feelings toward the Troy Paxons of the world is directly related to its ambivalence toward capitalism in general. Most of the world today embraces this economic system because it seems to work pretty well and because a more effective alternative does not appear to exist. The largest competing model, state ownership of businesses, seems to be a gigantic 20th century experiment that failed. But despite capitalism's "victory," most of the world does not accept much of its ideology nor some of its specific manifestations. Financial dealers are at the core of these issues.

People who are enthusiastic about capitalism tend to believe in economic coordination through markets and dealers. Many of these people are suspicious of economic coordination achieved through managers and hierarchies or through leaders and shared visions. They remind us that the very nature of hierarchy encourages executives to feather their own nests instead of worrying about efficiency, stockholders, customers, or employees. They are also quick to point out that shared vision is a tool used by cult-creating fanatics. Markets and dealers, on the other hand, tend to decentralize economic decision making and put it in the hands of people who have the most relevant information. Power that is decentralized is less subject to abuse. Markets also do not need altruistic motives to make them work. In Adam Smith's famous example, the butcher does not provide people with meat because of charity but because he is trying to earn a buck.[2] The market takes care of the rest.

Over the centuries, people have looked at market ideology with suspicion for a number of reasons. First, it is not difficult to find situations where markets do allow for undue concentration of power, typically with few sellers and many buyers, and thus do not work well. But even more fundamentally, most people are not comfortable with sellers who are concerned only with their own financial gain. We do not want butchers to literally weigh the cost of sanitary facilities against the cost of lawsuits or lost business if customers are hurt by a contaminated product. We worry that a butcher who cares only for money will, in a severe shortage of product, sell all his meat at very high prices to rich people, leaving us with nothing to eat. When this logic is applied to late 20th century financial dealers, the concern is that these people sometimes create transactions that are not necessarily in other people's or society's best interests. And unlike the butcher, by taking a small percentage of very large transactions, dealers can make huge incomes.

How widespread are these concerns? How legitimate are they? Consider for the moment the following exercise. 115 Class of '74 Harvard MBAs are asked to describe their biggest professional accomplishments between 1974 and 1991. Their statements are edited to provide clarifying detail, to make them more similar in style and length, and to downplay obvious exaggerations. Five current MBA students at Harvard Business School and two masters degree candidates at Harvard's Kennedy School of Government are then each given all 115 statements (a forty-five page document) and asked two questions: 1) How large a contribution to society has each person made with his or her biggest business accomplishment? 2) If you had the authority, how much income would you allow each of these people to make?

I actually did this little exercise in the spring of 1993. The seven students each spent about eight hours answering the questions and providing a rationale for their responses. As one might expect, they gave a range of opinions, but the rationales applied to generate scores were remarkably consistent: the more that the "biggest accomplishments" seemed to do something useful for customers (more or better products and services), employees (more and better jobs), stockholders (better returns on their investments), and the community (more tax dollars, better environment), the higher were *both* the social contribution and the deserved income scores.* As a result, there is usually a central tendency to the answers, and the overall pattern of the responses is very interesting.

On a −10 to +10 scale, only one of the 115 received an average social contribution score that was negative, and then only by a very small amount (−0.10). The typical class member received a score of +3.05. The fact that the Kennedy School students did not give lower social contribution numbers than the Business School

---

*The correlation between social contribution and deserved income scores was +0.723.

students suggests that these results are not unrealistically biased to the high side by a sympathetic group of judges.

As they relate to financial deal makers, results need to be reviewed with the following background. The dealers in the group made more money than their classmates in 1991: median total income of $280,000 versus $160,000 for others. They also had higher net worths: median wealth of $1,500,000 versus $870,000. Viewed against these facts, the opinions of the Class of '93 are intriguing. The current students gave the financial dealers somewhat lower social contribution scores than their Class of '74 peers. On a −10 to +10 scale, the typical dealer received a mean score of 2.04. Others were given a mean score of 3.48 (Exhibit 7.1). On average, the students also recommended that the financial dealers receive less income than the others: $130,298 versus $175,714 (see Exhibit 7.2).

The results of this exercise are even more dramatic if we focus on financial dealers versus leaders and on the highest and lowest numbers. Among the bottom 10% of social contribution scores, dealers outnumber leaders nearly four to one. Among the top 10% of scores, the exact opposite is true; leaders dominate dealers by four to one.*

EXHIBIT 7.1

Social Contribution: Financial Dealers Versus All Others

†Social contribution scores given by a panel of five Class of '93 MBAs and two Class of '93 Kennedy School Masters students

---

*The leaders with low social contribution scores include two people who were judged to be building businesses that benefited them but few others and one who was judged to be engaged in questionable business practices.

## EXHIBIT 7.2

### "Deserved" Versus Real Income

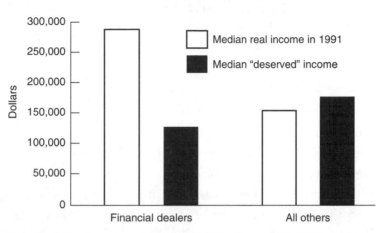

"Deserved" income given by a panel of five Class of '93 MBAs and two Class of '93 Kennedy School Masters students

Two caveats are important in viewing the statistics in Exhibits 7.1 and 7.2. First, many factors could be distorting these numbers.* Second, not all financial dealers received low social contribution and deserved income scores. Those whose activities seemed clearly to be connected to making firms more competitive or to helping firms grow often were judged very favorably. A dealer who built a fairly large and successful business by buying firms was given one of the very highest social contribution scores. But dealer numbers were pulled down by about a third of that group, 8% of the overall class, who were judged as making little social contribution and yet receiving very high salaries.[†] No other identifiable subgroup within the HBS Class of '74 looks even remotely like those people. In this exercise, consultants are described as over-paid too, but only a fraction as much as these dealers. Consultant social contribution scores are also much higher. The least econom-

---

*For example, perhaps something about financial dealers led them to do a poorer job than their classmates at explaining their biggest accomplishments in terms of the contribution to others.

[†]This group received average social contribution scores in this exercise of 1.28.

ically successful in the class are given social contribution scores that are low, but their more modest incomes are judged to be reasonably in line with their contributions. A few of the financial dealers stand out, one might say, like sore thumbs.

————————

To some degree, the concern with deal makers is driven by jealousy and by a lack of understanding of what they do. In my experience, the more that individuals understand the nature of a Phase III economy and the useful role that dealers can play in it, and the more that those same individuals are not unhappy with their own incomes, the less they tend to be critical of financial dealers. Also, the more that people have actually seen dealers help make firms more competitive, or have seen them donate huge amounts of money to charitable organizations, the more favorable the assessment.

Nevertheless, it is interesting that critical remarks are sometimes even made by the dealers themselves. In 1987, Warren Tolinghouse wrote: "I have achieved most of what I desired financially in a career. But I have failed to find meaningful work. So much of what I do seems of trivial importance or of little real value. At first, back in the 1970s, the sheer challenge of doing deals, doing them well, and doing them bigger was exciting and meaningful. It no longer is. Sometimes I wonder if we don't massively misallocate resources. It's a very depressing thought."

Most dealers do not sound like Tolinghouse. Most feel that they are engaged in important activities and use the logic of Adam Smith and economics to justify those actions. "If I were not providing others with value," says one, "I would not receive much business and the resulting high income." Some even bristle when phases like "social contribution" are used, since those words conjure up for them horribly failed socialist experiments in the former USSR, China, and elsewhere. In this regard, their attitudes are different from those of the typical person in the class, but only in a matter of degree. Virtually all of the 115 believe in markets. But some of the dealers treat market ideology like a religion. Virtually all of these MBAs are competitive, but some dealers are very, very competitive.[3] These differences in degree are nevertheless important, for they can sometimes lead to very different actions.

It is often taken for granted that many people on Main Street believe that there is something wrong with the U.S. or the world financial system. It is also assumed that MBAs from elite schools think that system is just fine, mostly because it serves well their own interests. The former may be true, but the latter is not. People in both the Class of '74 and the Class of '93, including some of the dealers themselves, also have reservations about how financial markets are working. They worry that some transactions serve no socially useful purpose, add no value, and exist only because a small number of people get rich.* They are also concerned that some deals actually undermine the capacity of firms to compete, and that too much talent is wasted in financial deal-maker jobs.†

In a 1991 interview, John Haggerty told me: "I am very angry that people in my class have done deals during the last decade of which they should be ashamed. I find it hard to believe that we sat in the same rooms and learned such different lessons. The manipu-

---

*Even Stan Roberts believes that useless transactions occur. But he says that 99% of the time this is not the case. Some of his non-dealer classmates think that socially harmful transactions are much more common.

†The story of Roberts' success, and of the success of other people like him, has had a noticeable effect on elite universities. Hordes of very talented young people have looked to the future and seen investment banking. It has been claimed, for example, that 40% of Yale's Class of '86 applied for jobs at one investment bank, First Boston.[4] At Harvard Business School recently, well over half the class has considered similar careers. Investment banking has been popular since at least the early 1970s. But interest in that industry has grown to huge proportions in the last decade. In the group of MBAs I taught in 1993, there were very few individuals who did not, at some point, seriously think that investment banking might be the best career for them.

lation of numbers and projections to justify almost any financial means or any financial end is wrong. I've seen extremely avaricious behavior. Some people seem to have had no counterbalancing feeling for the lives they were disrupting or the costs that were going to be borne as a result of the things they did. Now, the rest of us have to pick up the pieces. Perhaps some of this behavior is inevitable in a capitalist system. But if those irresponsible actions are coming from people with graduate degrees from a respected institution like Harvard, something is not right."

The vast majority of Haggerty's classmates want to make a contribution to society, and they see themselves as doing so through their work.* By producing needed products and services, employing people, paying taxes, building businesses, turning around businesses, helping fund startups, and providing leadership to economic organizations, they feel they add real value to society. Although some probably delude themselves about the size of their contributions, I doubt if most do.† Virtually all of them feel they could make more income if money were their only objective, but it is not. They want a happy family life, which most feel they have achieved, and they want to do something useful in their careers. When others accuse them of caring only for money and making little social contribution, often because of the bad press generated by those who take advantage of market and regulatory imperfections, they become frustrated and angry.

More than a few in the class have strong feelings on this subject. They believe that a few deal makers have poisoned the community well.

---

*They spend almost no time, on average, in civic, political, nonprofit, or religious activities. They concentrate on work, family, and themselves.

†Precisely measuring social contribution and the value they add through work is an impossible task. The conclusion I draw here is a judgment based on a great deal of information collected over a long period of time.

## NEW RULE #6

Today's global business environment offers huge opportunities for financially oriented deal makers. The new rule is: deal if you can, but be careful. Some of those opportunities are not in anyone's best interests except the deal maker's. Because some people are capitalizing on those socially questionable possibilities, the public is increasingly looking at all financial deal makers (and, to a lesser degree, all business people) with suspicion and contempt.

# PART III

# UNDERPINNINGS

# 8

## COMPETITIVE DRIVE

UNLESS YOU ARE A VERY LUCKY PERSON, YOU WILL NOT SUCCEED AT work today without an understanding of where the opportunities lie. But as important as that is, knowledge by itself is obviously not sufficient. Successfully implementing a career as an entrepreneur, consultant, leader, or dealer requires certain talents and attitudes. And once again, the experiences of the Class of '74 are very instructive in this regard.

Stan Roberts, Kevin Johnson, and almost all their classmates were born between 1944 and 1950.* They are at the front end of a demographic tidal wave that has been changing everything in its path for over four decades now. Their sheer numbers caused thousands of new elementary and secondary schools to be built in the

---

*Two were born in 1940, one in '41, one in '42, five in '43, ten in '44, eleven in '45, twenty-three in '46, eleven in '47, eighteen in '48, seventeen in '49, fifteen in '50, and one in '51.

1950s. In the 1960s, they fueled a great expansion of colleges and universities. In 1968, their resistance to the war in Vietnam helped stop Lyndon Johnson from seeking a second full term as President. It also helped elect Richard Nixon, who then resigned in disgrace just two months after the 115 finished graduate school.

In many ways, these individuals are far more diverse than popular stereotypes would suggest.* John Vrojic was a champion swimmer and spent thousands of hours in his youth training for competition. Bill Frazer never participated seriously in any sports and always felt that athletes were a slightly subhuman species. Bob Kruger grew up with an extraordinarily close relationship with his father; even now they see each other often and obviously enjoy each other's company a great deal. Carl Thomas has difficulty talking about his father without becoming visibly angry. Tony Michels fought in Vietnam, was proud of his military service then, and is still proud today. Rudolf Vogler wore his hair at shoulder length and marched in dozens of protests against the war in 1969 and 1970. Some in the class are very straightlaced; yet one has worked as a professional comedian. A few look like the "successful businessmen" central casting would send to a movie set; but at least 10% of them, possibly more, do not look even remotely like our stereotype of an MBA. They are tall and short, handsome and not so handsome, sophisticated and simple in their tastes. But despite all the differences, almost all are alike in a few ways. And those commonalities brought them in 1972 to Harvard Business School.

As is typical of people who receive graduate education from prestigious universities, most of these individuals spent their childhoods in generally favorable economic circumstances.† Half were raised in upper middle class homes. Only 13% came from the lower middle class; less than 1% had lower class parents.[1] 85% of their families made over $6,000 a year in 1960 compared to about 45% of all U.S. households.[2] The same pattern holds for formal

---

*On some dimensions they are very homogeneous. Most are male (93%), white (94%), and American (85%).

†For more detail on their socio-economic origins, see Notes 1–5.

schooling. Less than 10% of U.S. men had a college education or better versus 56% of Class of '74 dads.[3] In terms of occupation, their fathers were three times as likely to be managers and professionals than the average working man in 1960.[4]

For the most part, affluence was new to these families. The job, income, and educational levels of parents were higher than those of grandparents. The typical grandfather received twelve years of formal education, the typical father fifteen. In constant dollars, the average parent at age sixty had a net worth over three times as large as that of his or her own parents.[5] Many of the families rose from middle to upper middle class. About 70% were upwardly mobile by some measure.

Attitudes associated with upward mobility and striving appear to have been passed on from mothers and fathers to most Class of '74 children. Using a list of thirteen items that the National Opinion Research Council has given to a sample of the whole U.S. population with the question "What is desirable in a child?" I asked all 115 MBAs how much each of those factors was stressed by their parents. A comparison of the rankings produced by the population at large versus the Class of '74 shows a number of similarities. The two biggest differences: Class of '74 parents were said to have placed a higher value on "trying hard to succeed" and a much higher value on "being a good student." (See Exhibit 8.1) They also placed somewhat less emphasis on obeying them as parents, being considerate of others, and having self-control. This kind of value environment could produce very self-centered individuals. But it could also create highly motivated people who are willing to challenge the rules of the game.

Parental values appear to have been a powerful force in most of their lives. Nearly half say their fathers were "highly influential." Slightly more say the same about their mothers. Most also report that their fathers were important role models.*

---

*53% report that fathers were important role models. Those from upper middle class families were much more likely to respect dad as a role model than those from lower middle class families.

## EXHIBIT 8.1

### Rank Order of Values Stressed by Parents

|  | The 115 Class of '74 MBAs | Sample of U.S. Population (1972-1982)* |
|---|:---:|:---:|
| Being honest | 1 | 1 |
| Being responsible | 2 | 4 |
| *Being a good student* | 3 | *12* |
| *Trying hard to succeed* | 4 | *9* |
| Having good sense and sound judgment | 5 | 2 |
| Obeying parents | 6 | 3 |
| Having good manners | 7 | 6 |
| Being considerate of others | 8 | 5 |
| Being neat and clean | 9 | 11 |
| Having self-control | 10 | 7 |
| Being interested in how and why things happen | 11 | 8 |
| Getting along with other children | 12 | 10 |
| Acting like a boy (if male) or a girl (if female) | 13 | 13 |

*Data adapted from a NORC survey regarding "What is desirable in a child." See Pages 115–118 in *General Social Surveys*, 1972-1982: Cumulative Codebook, produced by National Opinion Research Center, University of Chicago

The exact nature of parent-child relationships and the methods used to transmit values vary within the group. In some cases, parents were classic role models. By watching them work to excel, and by identifying with them, children learned to "try hard to suc-ceed." In other cases, parents aggressively set tough standards for their children and competed with them. "My father was never pleased," reports one member of the class. "Nothing I did was ever right. It could always have been done better. I scored ten points in my first varsity basketball game in high school and his comment was, 'Why only ten points?'" In still other cases, the value of finan-cial independence was brought home in more direct ways. When he was eight years old, one member of the class was taken by his father to visit the factory where he was employed. "He wanted to show me where he had to work all day so that I would never want to end up doing what he did. The message was clear: working in that kind of environment is a nasty, dirty job."

Although the members of the Class of '74 say that they are like their fathers and mothers in many ways, one can clearly see a sig-nificant generational difference. Having lived through the Great Depression and then World War II, their parents are often some-what wary of markets, competition, and wide open capitalism while being basically optimistic about government and bureau-cracy. The comparable experiences for the Class of '74 were the 1950s boom and the Vietnam War, which left them with just the opposite inclinations. Children usually saw the economic good times after World War II as a product of markets or competition and the Vietnam/Watergate disasters as a consequence of central-ized authority. As a result, parents often behaved in ways that have been labeled "patriotic"—they bought Buicks because they were good American cars. Their children often acted more "self-centered"—they bought Hondas and were confident that competi-tion would force Detroit to get better.

Another way in which these generational differences have mani-fested themselves is around the issue of security. As Bill Windsor said in a 1992 interview: "My father was very much a corporate manager in the traditional style of someone at IBM or General Motors, someone who expects to have a lifetime career with the firm and does. Maybe he was a victim of the Depression, but he al-ways went on about security and about working for a 'good' company (by which he meant a large and well-established American firm). I am like my father in so many ways, but in that respect, I'm totally different. Security is the least important thing to me."

Security has been of little importance to virtually everyone in the class.* Meeting high standards, competing, and winning have been important.

———

Alan Martin's background is fairly typical. His paternal grandfather was a farmer. His mother's father was a salesman. Alan's father achieved more occupationally than either of them. Mr. Martin had a college degree and worked in an ad agency. For most of Alan's childhood, his father was an account executive with an income nearly double the national average. Mrs. Martin also had a few years of college and had worked until Alan, the first of three children, was born. Important in much of Alan's upbringing was an attitude that he should continue this upwardly mobile tradition. Getting the same education and the same job as his father was not sufficient. More was expected. "This idea was communicated in both subtle and not so subtle ways," Alan reported in a 1979 interview. "Part of it was simply dad as an example or role model. Part of it was my mother's reaction to report cards. The implied philosophy was that we were fortunate to have what we had and we shouldn't just coast to maintain it. Since I grew up with more privileges than my parents, I should achieve greater things. I think that as they received more and more evidence that I was pretty smart, they raised the bar higher and higher. By the time I was in junior high school, they were clearly treating me differently than my younger brother, who has somewhat less natural talent. They

———

*More recent MBAs at Harvard have filled out an instrument developed by Dr. Tim Butler called the Management and Professional Reward Value Profile. On a scale of 1 (low) to 12 (high), the average score for "security" for these MBAs has been less than 2!

# ALAN MARTIN

BUSINESS EXPERIENCE

First National Bank of Los Angeles
- Senior Vice President, Capital Markets (1990–1993)
- Vice President, Capital Markets (1982–1990)

P & S Supermarkets, Los Angeles, California
- Vice President of Finance (1980–1982)
- Treasurer (1978–1980)
- Finance Manager (1977–1978)

First National Bank of Los Angeles
- Assistant Loan Officer (1975–1977)
- Trainee (1974)

First American Food Stores, Boston, Massachusetts
- Financial Analyst (1970–1972)

EDUCATION

Harvard Business School, Boston, Massachusetts.
- Masters in Business Administration, 1974.

Columbia University, New York, New York.
- B.S. in Business Administration, 1970.

PERSONAL

Background: Born in 1948, raised in Connecticut. One younger brother. Father worked in an advertising agency, mother was not employed outside the home.

Marital Status: Married in 1978 to Barbara Calloway (managing director for large retail business). Two children, ages 10 and 8.

expected both of us to strive to use our abilities to the maximum, but since I seemed to have more potential, they expected more of me."

In 1992, when attempting to explain his professional success (see profile on previous page), Alan talked about a large number of factors including luck. But he gave no element greater weight than the high standards, ideals, and ambitions that started with his parents. "I'm a pretty determined person," he says with a straight face while his wife howls in laughter and tells a story about how he bent four golf clubs around a tree after finishing third in a relatively unimportant tournament. "I do not completely understand where that comes from. But part of it is clearly related to my parents and the way they raised me. There is no question about that."

Upwardly mobile values usually came from fathers and mothers, but not exclusively. In David Webber's case, an uncle was of great importance. David was born and raised in Connecticut, the first of four children of a small businessman and his wife. He attended college at the University of Iowa where he was student body president and a member of the swimming team. During his college summers, he worked at a wholesaling and trading business that had been founded by an uncle. "I went into New York City thinking they were going to give me a job in the stockroom because I was only eighteen years old. Instead, they gave me a plane ticket to London. I quickly realized that there was a big and interesting world out there."

Upon graduation from Iowa, Webber went directly to Harvard Business School. "I remember our first accounting paper," he said in 1991. "I turned it in and got a D—with a note at the bottom to see the professor. When I went in to see him, he asked what I had studied as an undergraduate. I told him it was philosophy. He said my paper was a great philosophy paper, so I asked him if he wanted to change the grade. He said, 'I'm sorry. This is accounting, not philosophy. You've got the whole idea wrong.' I thought, 'How the hell am I supposed to know this?' We had only been there three weeks. He said, 'Look, if I were you, I'd give serious thought about dropping out of this program, because I don't think you can do it here.'" Webber still remembers that incident as one of the lowest points in his life.

He did not drop out, nor even consider the possibility very seriously. During his second year, David did think long and hard about his career options and eventually chose to return to his uncle's business, but with some misgivings. "At that time, the alternatives looked so much more glamorous than this little, low-tech, distribution business. And my uncle offered no guarantees. He made it clear that he was not running a 'family business.' If you can't perform, you're out."

David began his post-HBS career as an assistant to one of the firm's officers. He then spent the next few years traveling around the world trying to develop additional markets for the company and additional sources of supply. In the Far East—Korea, Japan, Taiwan—he helped open offices for the firm. In Africa and Latin America, he helped complete major business deals. It was quite exotic, exciting, and very educational. Globalization of the firm's businesses created many new risks, but also new opportunities.

By 1977, Webber had proved himself sufficiently that he was made a vice president. In 1978, he took over responsibility for one of the company's divisions and supervised its fifty employees. In 1980, after a major downturn in one of the firm's most important businesses, he created a new income stream in a short period of time—"a very wild and exhilarating experience." In 1981, he became a senior vice president and started racing sailboats. In 1983, he was named the number two person at the firm, and in 1984, he became president and gained a significant equity interest in the business. He also got married that year (like many of the most successful people in his class, David delayed creating a family until he was firmly established in his career). In 1986, he was given the additional title of CEO and became a father (see profile on next page).

Throughout the 1980s, Webber's business expanded and even began to develop a manufacturing capability for some of its key

# DAVID WEBBER

WORK EXPERIENCE

Berringer Industrial Corp.                    Cleveland, Ohio
- President and CEO (1986–1993)
- President (1984–1986)
- Chief Operating Officer (1983–1984)
- Senior Vice President (1981–1983)
- Vice President and Head of European Operations (1978–1981)
- Trader (1975–1977)
- Trainee (1974)

EDUCATION

Harvard Business School                    Boston, Massachusetts
Masters in Business Administration, 1974.

University of Iowa                              Iowa City, Iowa
B.A. in Philosophy, 1972.  President of student body.

PERSONAL

Background:  Born in 1946, raised in Connecticut.  First of 4 children.  Father owned a small business, mother was not employed outside the home.

Marital Status:  Married Lucy Weingarten in 1984.  Four children, ages 7, 5, 3, and 1.

Quote: "Whatever I do, I plan not to be mediocre.  In my career, I want to make a name for myself and I want to be able to live as I choose.  I will not be satisfied as a good middle manager or vice president.  I want to be president. (1974)"

wholesale and trading products. At a time when some businesses have run into major problems, his firm grew over 1,000%, from $58 million in 1974 to $600 million in 1992. It is now the largest privately held company in its industry in the world.

When asked why he has done so well in business, David talks first about how he deals with people. "I always like to make 49¢ and let the other guy make 51. Then when he wants to do business again, he'll come back to me." He also readily admits his uncle has played an important part in his success. But as he sees it, the family-like business and the privilege it implies are not the real issues. "My uncle is very driven and very focused. He became important in my life when my mother moved next door to him at the end of my last year in high school. My father had just died and Uncle George ended up spending a lot of time with my family. When he arrived, I was about to go to the University of Iowa. One of my brothers was on a track that took him to Calargo College, my sister was on a track that took her to Western Michigan University, and my youngest brother was having psychological problems. After my uncle had spent four or five years being an important part of our lives, I ended up at Harvard Business School, one brother transferred to Princeton, my sister transferred to Amherst, and my youngest brother got into Yale. It is amazing how his zip got into all of us. I think it was a question of traffic signals."

Traffic signals were important to virtually all 115 of them. For most, the message communicated by the lights appears to have been simple: you are expected to succeed.

———————

A strong drive to excel rarely sustains itself in youngsters without much reinforcement. For David Webber and his classmates, this usually came first from parents and then from schools. The quality of their elementary and secondary schooling varied, with those from richer backgrounds generally offered a better education. But in a very broad sense, almost all of them appear to have been served well by their formal instruction.

From an early age, they were put in academic competitions which they mostly won—month after month, year after year. Even today, Jerry Portas remembers dominating his peers in his youth, despite not being the smartest student. By the time he reached junior high school, he was in classes with many intelligent children, yet he still outperformed most of them. Winning produced self-confidence, which became a part of his expectations, maybe even a part of his character.

Like Jerry, most of the 115 MBAs would have successfully taken hundreds of tests before reaching the age of eighteen. By the time they entered high school, almost all were in special classes that were more challenging than the normal fare. Despite the competition, they usually did well. Nearly all left home to go to reasonably well-known colleges and universities.[6] Again, despite the competition, one half graduated in the top 10% of their classes.[7] Along the way, they learned a great deal—sometimes because they had an inherent love of learning, sometimes because good education was a by-product of doing well in school.

In both high school and college, most participated in some form of extracurricular activity which broadened their abilities. Eighty-seven percent were in social or academic clubs. Like David Webber, most were members of the student government, usually competing and winning to obtain these positions. Over half were on varsity teams. Many were on yearbook/newspaper staffs or were in musical/dramatic groups.[8] For the most part, they participated in these ways because they were sociable, liked group activities, found competition to be fun, and believed such engagement would be helpful on their résumés.

Academically, few focused on either esoteric or easy subjects. The most popular college major was some form of engineering. A third of them received those degrees versus 6% of all collegians their age. Another 18% majored in economics, a specialty chosen by only 2% of college graduates back then.[9] There are very few art history majors in this group, and none obtained degrees in subjects where the competition was nonexistent or very easy.*

After college, the typical Class of '74 MBA worked for two years. A third ended up in the military, mostly as a consequence of the Vietnam War. Virtually all had demanding positions of some sort.

Business school attracted them for a number of reasons. Because they had done well in school, graduate education was a logical option. Although few if any qualified as intellectuals, with a typical score of 625 out of 800 on the Graduate Management Admissions Test, they were certainly analytically capable.[10] Most were also very ambitious. The aspiration to run a business or be a millionaire some day was not uncommon. They clearly liked the economic, power, and status rewards that might be available in a successful business career.†

The Harvard Business School application form was intimidating. Not only did they have to supply transcripts, records of extracurricular activities and work experience, plus recommendations, they also had to write lengthy answers to a number of essay questions: describe your three most substantial accomplishments and explain why you view them as such; what factors led you to decide that this program would be most helpful to your career development? discuss the vocations or professions, other than administration, which you may have seriously considered; give a candid evaluation of yourself discussing those characteristics you feel have become your strengths and those you feel are your weaknesses; describe a situation or job in which you felt you had some responsibility and tell us what you learned from the experience. Some spent over a hundred hours trying to get their applications into winning form.

When they arrived in Boston in September 1972, few had a

---

*For more detailed statistics about their colleges, college performance, extracurricular activities, and majors, see Notes 6–9.

†For more detailed statistics on values, attitudes, and GMAT scores, see Notes 10 and 11.

clear vision of the specific kind of business career they would pursue. But most seem to have shared a dream.[12] One of them described it this way: "I want to be successful at work, both in my own eyes and in the eyes of others. Success means money, status, influence, and an interesting job, all achieved by working hard at some useful economic activity. A successful career means using my skills and abilities to the utmost, but not in a job that ruins my family life, or hurts others." In addition to this, some wanted to accumulate great wealth, many wished to run a business, and a few felt very strongly about making the world a better place. In terms of specifics, many had no idea what industry or type of company would best suit them. But almost all had a sense that they were moving forward on the right path. Getting into a good graduate school was another win in what they hoped would continue to be a very winning life.

---

In their MBA program, they found an intellectually challenging and competitive environment which, years later, most reported was more difficult, more worthwhile, but less enjoyable than previous educational experiences.[13] During the first few months, they worked hard trying to master what seemed at times like an overwhelming amount of material. Some worked every night to 12:00 or 1:00 A.M. and still did not complete all their homework. They also received little feedback or personalized attention from the faculty. Some seriously wondered if they would survive under those conditions.

Ted Levitt taught the required marketing course that year to half of the 115. A creative professional and guru in his field, Levitt was born in 1925 in Vollmerz, Germany. He came to the United States in 1935, received a Ph.D. in economics at Ohio State in 1951, and joined the Harvard faculty in 1959. As an instructor, he was both tough and charismatic. Members of the Class of '74 met him when he walked into a classroom on September 14, 1972, the very first day of the term. Tim Bonigan describes the scene in this way: "Without introducing himself or the course, Levitt focused his eyes on a guy in the third row and said 'Mr. Hodson, will you please begin.' Unsure as to what he should do next, Jerry [Hodson] began awkwardly talking about the case we had read for that class. Levitt went after him without mercy, pointing out factual errors, logical inconsistencies, unjustified assumptions, and much more. Twenty-five minutes later, Jerry was sitting in a pool of his own sweat, and the rest of us were paying a great deal of attention to Professor Levitt."

For five months, Levitt hammered away at them. They reciprocated by competing vigorously to do well in his eyes. After teaching what he considered to be good work habits, he focused on instructing them about "responsibility." He constantly asked individuals what they would do if they were a specific manager in the case under discussion and always pushed the consequences of their decisions back in their faces. He taught marketing more by induction than deduction—getting them to look and think many times before encouraging generalizations. He also taught much more than just marketing in a narrow sense. He instructed them about business in general, about life on earth in the 20th century, and about the nature of managerial jobs. As they grew to respect him more and more, his own beliefs probably became very influential.

Over a two year period, they took a total of twenty-two courses and had twenty-one other instructors in addition to Levitt. A few had C. Roland Christensen, a man who was fast becoming a legend in his own time. Others had memorable individuals like Bob Anthony, Tony Athos, John McArthur, Wic Skinner, and Paul Vatter. All of these men were great teachers and, like Levitt, taught much more than just business in a narrow sense.

The second year was less intense; for most, it was a time of decision regarding next steps in their careers. During the spring of 1974, the average person interviewed for ten jobs, received four offers, and then accepted one paying the then princely sum of $18,000 per year. They were between twenty-three and thirty-four years old at the time of graduation. About half were married. Many had educational debts to repay. All had high hopes for the future.

It is difficult to determine what influence the MBA program had on these people. Overall, it seems to have built mostly on preexisting strengths.[14] The students added new knowledge to their memory banks: information about marketing and finance, about analytical tools and conceptual frameworks, about dozens of different industries, and more. They strengthened some skill areas: the ability to think rigorously, to distill complicated issues down to key factors, to communicate clearly. They added potentially useful acquaintances and friends to their contact networks: fellow students, faculty, and business executives who visited campus regularly. They received a major reinforcement for their beliefs in the efficacy of markets and competition. Perhaps the single biggest subliminal message in the curriculum was that Markets and Competition are GOOD. They also obtained the Harvard stamp-of-approval, giving access to more jobs and more companies than had been available to them previously. Firms saw the degree as a signal that these people possessed traits such as intelligence and drive.[15]

But most of all, they acquired even more self-confidence in their growing abilities. They had been tested under tough conditions and done just fine, thank you. The fears that many of them had about competing during the first few months of the MBA program turned out to be unjustified. The experience told them that they could handle pressure and many difficult demands. As Tom Wells said in a 1979 interview: "After you have been to a place like that and survived, the world looks less intimidating and opportunities look less risky and difficult. I think your own aspirations often seem, perhaps, too low. You say to yourself, if I did OK under these tough conditions, then maybe nearly anything is possible."

———————

At one level, their life experiences did a poor job of preparing them for the post '73 economic environment. They were raised in an era of almost steady growth. They learned little directly about tough economic times. Their elementary, secondary, and undergraduate schooling focused more on the past than on the future, and for very understandable reasons. The past is known, can be studied, and thus can be taught. The future is murky, debatable, and difficult to study. Even Harvard Business School did little to teach them about areas of increasing opportunity: small business, entrepreneurship, leadership, and non-manufacturing industries like consulting. The MBA program focused more on what had been a source of opportunity in the past: professional management in big industrial businesses.

But despite all this, in a far more fundamental sense, their early life experiences did help prepare them for the economic environment in which they have worked. The hallmark of that environment is global competition. And these people have systematically developed into strong competitors.

From their earliest years, their experiences taught most of them that competition is good and fun. This was true in academics, in sports, in student government. Over time, they became more and more self-confident in competitive situations and more willing to set high goals and to take risks. At both conscious and preconscious levels, they embraced the belief that competitive systems are proper and just. The cultural revolution of the late 1960s challenged, and often modified, the more extreme versions of these beliefs. But for most of these MBAs, the era of hippies did not fundamentally alter their faith in competition. If anything, Watergate and Vietnam reinforced their skepticism toward big centralized bureaucracies.

From the beginning of their lives, they have also been developing the personal assets needed to compete effectively. The list is a long one: healthy bodies, good minds, a solid education, useful role models, a track record of achievements, many potentially helpful friends and acquaintances, and self-confidence. Both their parents and educators were very helpful in this regard. Parents taught them to try to win and gave them valuable tools for competition. School systems put them in an endless series of competitive events and gave the winners recognition and access to the best educational opportunities. By the spring of 1974, their bank accounts may have been almost empty, but their human capital accounts were overflowing.

In combination, the competitive drive and the personal assets have helped equip these people to locate lucrative possibilities in the turbulent post '73 economic environment, to develop the additional skills needed to exploit these opportunities, and then to win. Few found a Phase III economy to be easy. At times, it was surprising, depressing, and painful for most of them. But their self-confidence, determination, and competitive drive helped them deal with failures both on and off the job. Circumstances that can immobilize people simply did not stop the majority of them. This is especially true for the most successful in the class.

Virtually none of the 115 sets low goals or is lackadaisical about

EXHIBIT 8.2

Competitive Drive and 1992 Earnings

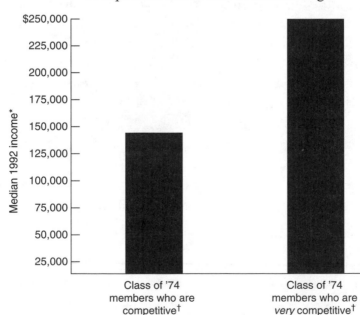

*Includes bonuses and equity appreciation for entrepreneurs
†Based on a battery of psychological tests taken in 1973 by 59 of the 115.

accomplishing goals. But some are clearly more competitive than others. And those who both set higher standards and want more strongly to win are doing better economically than their other classmates (see Exhibit 8.2).[16] Indeed, of the 200 personality and background factors on which I have information, nothing, including childhood socioeconomic class[17] and intelligence,[18] relates more to income differences within the group than competitive drive (see Exhibits 8.3 and 8.4). On average, those with both more ambitious goals and a stronger desire to achieve those goals are also more satisfied with their work lives than are the rest of their peers.*

Although movement into a new economic era that looks more like Phase II could alter the relationship shown in Exhibit 8.2, that

EXHIBIT 8.3

## Parental Affluence and 1991 Earnings
## of Class of '74 Children

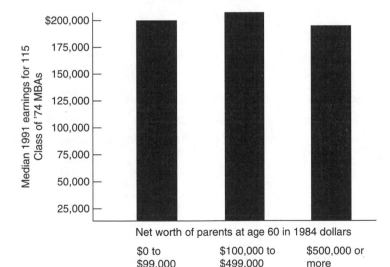

Note: Includes bonuses and equity appreciation for entrepreneurs

---

*Among those in the class who are least satisfied with their work in 1990 and 1991, "competitive" members outnumber the "very competitive" four to one. Among the most satisfied are an equal number from both groups.

EXHIBIT 8.4

## GMAT Scores and 1991 Earnings

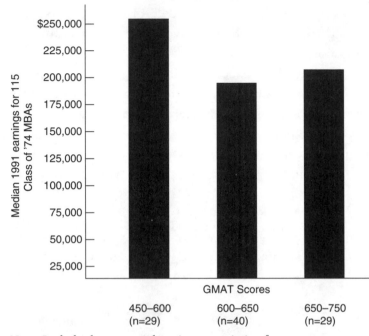

Note: Includes bonuses and equity appreciation for entrepreneurs

change is unlikely anytime in the foreseeable future.[19] From everything I have seen in this and in other studies, at least in the near term, competitive drive will continue to play an important role in economic success.

---

### NEW RULE #7

In the increasingly competitive and fast-moving global business environment, winners reap big rewards while those who are unable or unwilling to compete can encounter huge problems. The new rule is: you have got to be an able competitor. Effective competition requires many things, especially high standards and a strong desire to win.

# 9

---

# LIFELONG LEARNING

---

IN TODAY'S INCREASINGLY FAST-MOVING WORLD, JUST ABOUT EVERY-thing is becoming obsolete at a rate that is shocking compared to even the recent past. Business concepts, product designs, competitor intelligence, capital equipment, and all kinds of knowledge have shorter credible life spans. Firms and individuals rarely succeed when they are static and try to live off the past.

To understand why some people are doing so well today at work, one clearly needs to understand their career paths (Chapter 2), the economic environment in which they have operated (Chapter 3), the specific ways in which they have found opportunities in that environment (Chapters 4 through 7), and the kind of people they are (Chapter 8). But one additional factor is also very important: their willingness and ability to continue to learn and grow. The 115 Class of '74 MBAs were certainly very able when they left school. But their capabilities to make things happen in a difficult economic era have grown manyfold over the past twenty years. And that growth is centrally related to their success.

---

Harvard Business School has for decades specialized in general management more than finance, marketing, or some other business function. Back in 1972 and 1973, students were told that few of them would begin their careers in a generalist job, but that most would be promoted into that kind of work within two decades. A typical career path would start in an entry level marketing (or finance) position, move through a series of larger and larger marketing (or finance) assignments, and then shift into a number of increasingly bigger general management jobs. We recognized that not everyone would do this. A few would have more functionally mixed careers before moving permanently into general management and a few would remain always as specialists (in finance, marketing, etc.). But that would not be the norm.

The relevant career path data for the Class of '74 are summarized in Exhibit 9.1. By far the biggest category, representing half the group, is something few of us talked about back then. That category represents a less linear and more dynamic mixture of jobs. It means, for example, two finance positions followed by a marketing job, then a job in finance again, then a general management position, then another one in marketing. Sometimes these career paths are masked in résumés either because job titles do not convey the true nature of positions or because résumé writers fear reality looks too confusing or unorthodox. For the Class of '74, what had been considered unorthodox is now normal.

In a Phase II economic environment, careers for many people fit into a few simple categories and were reasonably linear in nature.* Increasingly in Phase III, this is no longer true—and not just for Harvard MBAs.[1] The shift is most directly related to the turbulent economic environment. Mergers, bankruptcies, downturns created by foreign competition, and new technologies are all creating much more volatility than thirty years ago. But for Class of '74 MBAs, this shift is also associated with their aggressive search for the growth opportunities that can equip them to suc-

---

*In large organizations in particular, careers were relatively static for most people (factory and office workers). Managerial careers tended to be linear progressions up a single functional ladder.

EXHIBIT 9.1

Career Paths for 115 Class of '74 MBAs

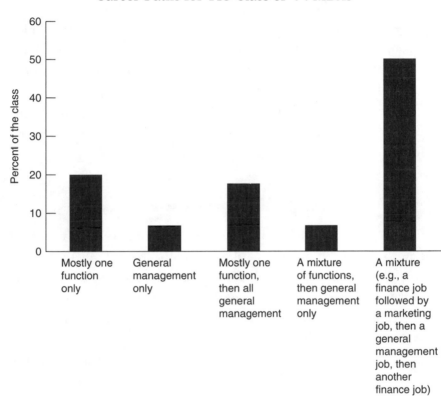

ceed in that turbulent environment. This pattern is very clear in the yearly correspondence with the class: "The assignment in Brazil was tough at first, but now it's clear it was a very good choice. I have grown much more in one year down here than in the prior five years in the U.S."; "Just successfully negotiated the sale of our division. Having never done anything quite like this, it was an incredible learning experience"; "It was tough getting this job, but because of it, the last four years have been a significant growth period for me, a movement from being just a financially oriented deal guy to being an administrator/manager/leader"; "The move I engineered into finance is going to pay off big in the long term. I now really understand. . . ."

In our traditional way of thinking about education, we talk as if learning is mostly over after the last degree is completed. For the Class of '74, this is not even remotely accurate. Non-linear career paths—sometimes created by the volatile times, sometimes explicitly sought as a source of learning, often a combination of the two—have been turned into major growth opportunities that have made them stronger and even more competitively able.

For many people, environmental turbulence has been annoying at best, often a source of dread. For most of these MBAs, that turbulence has been an important source of growth.

_____

Jack Bowen was raised in a small town in Indiana. He was a good but not outstanding student, played on the basketball team, and was active in his church's youth league. In 1966, he left home to attend Purdue, where he was active in a variety of extracurricular organizations and where he created a small movement called Christians Against the War In Vietnam. Upon graduation in 1970 with a degree in chemical engineering, he accepted a position at the San Francisco office of a firm that did both technical and management consulting. Two years later, he came to Harvard.

Fellow students in the MBA program remember Jack as a soft-spoken young man with a warm smile. "He was obviously a small town boy, relatively tall and thin, yet with a certain physical and emotional solidness to him," according to Kevin Johnson, "like a young Jimmy Stewart or Henry Fonda."

Jack spent his first ten years after graduate school in a large manufacturing firm before moving into a medium-sized manufacturing business (see profile on next page). His correspondence during that decade includes this item in 1978: "Major reorganization six months ago. Lots of uncertainty before and after. Have taken a sizable risk by requesting (and getting) a job in a newly created division. The opportunities and challenges will be big. At a

# JACK BOWEN

PROFESSIONAL

1985–1993          Chemcon Corporation                St. Louis, MO
- Executive Vice President (1989–1993)
- Senior Vice President, North American
  Sales (1985–1989)

1974–1985          Iron Industries                    Pittsburgh, PA
- Senior Vice President, Corporate (1984–1985)
- General Manager, President, Specialty Chemicals
  (1982–1984)
- Vice President Marketing and Administration,
  Specialty Chemicals (1978–1981)
- Marketing Manager, Specialty Chemical Division
  (1976–1978)
- Sales, Industrial Chemicals Division (1974–1976)

1970–1972          Arthur Johnson Consulting      San Francisco, CA
- Consultant

EDUCATION

1972–1974          Harvard Business School              Boston, MA
- Masters in Business Administration

1966–1970          Purdue University                  Lafayette, IN
- B.S. in Chemical Engineering

PERSONAL

Born in Elksville, Indiana in 1948. Oldest of three children. Father was a high school teacher, mother was a
senior non-clerical official in her church.

Married Mary Lou Durkin in 1975. Three children, ages
17, 15, and 12.

minimum, I'll learn a lot. Too early to tell if this was a mistake or not." In 1980, he writes: "Had a major confrontation with a subordinate. His performance was poor, partly because our business is getting tougher and tougher, partly because he refuses to change in light of new conditions. The whole episode was very painful, but we've now got him in a new job for which he seems better suited (and is doing well in so far), and I think I have matured a notch as a manager."

In 1982, Jack writes: "Promoted to division general manager. A big jump for me. Lots of pressure, especially since most of the corporation is doing poorly now." The story continues in 1983: "The challenge has been to get a group of people to raise their standards and really pull together, despite the uncertainty created by raids on our parent corporation. The hours have been too long at times, but I think I've grown a great deal."

The 1984 correspondence includes this: "I may have made a big mistake by leaving my division, which is operating so well, and moving to corporate. It's a mess here, but I think if I had stayed at the division, I would have gotten so entrenched and comfortable that I could end up retiring there. We'll see." In 1985: "It has truly been an incredible year. I took on three major projects, made good progress on all three, despite all the difficulties, then got into a conflict with the chairman. I sincerely believe that he is over his head and is killing the company. The last straw was a series of financial manipulations designed to keep buyers away, none of which are in the long-term best interests of the firm. All this forced me to reconsider my own goals and values, which was difficult, but I think very useful. Net result, I gave him an ultimatum, and then when it was clear I was never going to get him to do the right thing, I quit (or was fired, it's hard to say, probably a little of both). Not a happy time, but the more I think about this, the more confident I am that I did the right thing. I've already got a new job that looks terrific so far. And I think (hope) I am a lot more capable of handling the new experience because of what I endured last year."

Turbulence is common in business environments today. Literally millions of people are being buffeted by foreign competition, layoffs, mergers, and more. What is so interesting about Jack Bowen and people like him is their ability to turn a source of pain and problems into something useful.[2] New competition, raiders, reorganizations, and the like become not just destructive, but an important source of growth. Difficult events knock them out of their comfort zones and present new challenges. Because they are self-confident and competitive enough not to run away from these challenges, and because they are subsequently willing to look honestly at their successes and failures, they learn and grow. That growth, in turn, makes them more and more able to deal with the new economic environment.

Not all of the class has been as effective as Jack in growing over the past twenty years. For the most part, those who have grown very little are among the least successful members of the group.*

———————

David DeLong's life looks idyllic. He is the president of a company that has grown under his stewardship at over 35% per year for the past six years (see profile on next page). Because of his equity holdings, he has become a wealthy man. He is married and has two children for whom he obviously cares deeply. Ask about his family and career, and the story he will probably tell is about how he has been very fortunate, has had a good life, and is lucky enough to have a terrific family. It can sound somewhat like a 1990s version of a 1950s Ozzie and Harriet T.V. show.

An examination of David's yearly correspondence shows another side to this story. *1977:* "Brother had a nervous breakdown caused by a deteriorating marriage. I am very close to him. It hurt a great deal to see his life in such a mess. Over the last nine

———————

*Measuring "growth" is obviously very difficult. But in interviews conducted in 1992, people who talk about turbulent events and their learning from those events are more than twice as likely to be the top half of the group in terms of income or job title.

# DAVID DELONG

BUSINESS EXPERIENCE

Porter International, Restaurant Division                 Los Angeles, CA
- Chairman and CEO (1993)
- President and CEO (1988–1992)
- President and COO (1987)
- Executive Vice President (1986)

Paramount Foods                                            Boston, MA
Seafood Restaurant Division
- Senior Vice President, Marketing (1983–1985)
- Vice President of Operations, West Region (1981–1982)
- Director of Advertising (1980)

Paramount Foods, Cereals Division              New York, NY
- Product Manager, Cold Cereals (1977–1979)
- Assistant Product Manager, Cold Cereals (1975–1976)
- Assistant Product Manager, Warm Cereals (1974)

Stamford Public Schools                              Stamford, CT
- Math Teacher and President of Teachers' Association (1970–1972)
- Math Teacher (1968–1972)

EDUCATION

Harvard Business School                               Boston, MA
- Masters of Business Administration, 1974

University of Connecticut                               Storrs, CT
- B.S. in math, 1968

PERSONAL

Born in New Jersey in 1946, raised on the East Coast. Father owned a restaurant.

Married Elizabeth Arnold in 1980. Two children, ages 12 and 10.

months, I have devoted much time in trying to be of help. Spent my vacation with him, flew him to Chicago for a big party in his honor. It's been tough." *1978:* "Wife had a miscarriage. Much pain all around." *1979:* "Job of VP Marketing in Frozen Foods Division was given to a peer despite the fact that I was told I was #1 on the promotion list and that I would have first chance at any VP level jobs, especially in marketing." *1980:* "I took a big gamble with big stakes. Situation was bad, and I was ready to walk. Had a confrontation with boss over important mistakes he was making. Apparently others agreed and he was fired. I was then given a major promotion."

*1981:* "Mother was very sick. After a critical operation, new events developed every two weeks with me over 1,000 miles away. As all this coincided with me in a new job, it was the most stress I have ever been under. This, in turn, led to a crisis in my marriage. After struggling for over two months, we were able to redefine our relationship in terms of mutually agreed upon goals and then move forward. We took a 'getaway weekend,' later spent two weeks in Hawaii, and in general, things have been on the rebound ever since. In all, it's been a year of much personal growth. The three most important factors in my life (job, family, parents) all pulled at me at the same time. I put in twenty hour days at work sometimes and then spent the entire weekend with my mother or wife. If things had not improved, I don't know what I would have done. I do know this—I could not have gone on much longer without something giving."

*1983:* "Had a brief health scare. Think it was mostly due to stress." *1984:* "I was offered the job of president of our largest competitor with a terrific salary package. The decision was agonizing, because it would have meant going to the 'enemy' after four years of hard work helping to build our organization (hiring people, etc.). It was an awful thirty days, but finally said no." *1985:* "Crisis on both the job and in my marriage. On job, had serious differences with a key peer and perception of boss regarding job performance. It was a year of hell and I almost quit, almost was fired. Finally my peer was fired. I have now set to work trying to rebuild the department, performance, relationships, and so forth. All this put a severe strain on my marriage. Situation is not yet fully resolved." *1986:* "Two big events. I left the firm for which I had been working for $11\frac{1}{2}$ years. I chose a smaller and more entrepreneurial company. Wanted less bull and more direct involvement. Also, my sister has been sick and I have been trying to give her both financial and moral support." *1988:* "My father was operated on for cancer. He survived a difficult procedure and is in the process of beating tough odds." *1989:* "Father's illness continues, causing much stress and emotional pain." *1990:* "Father died and I miss him deeply."

*1991:* "My daughter was very sick during the year and spent two weeks in the hospital followed by surgery. Nothing hurts more than when your children are hurt. . . . My son has needed some strong parenting. He is bright and creative and struggles at times to fit into his conservative school. . . . The death of an HBS classmate's wife caught us all by surprise and reminds us of our vulnerability. . . . At work, an economic downturn is putting very tough pressures on the business."

*1992:* "My daughter had to have a second operation. Thank God she's OK now. . . . I dedicated a large portion of my spare time to my son—helping him in his schoolwork, playing golf and basketball with him, having him come to work with me, etc. . . . At work, had to terminate two senior employees. One was a fantastic person who just can't get the job done. Very very tough to do this."

We sometimes envy the people who achieve great economic success because they seem to have such carefree lives—full of positives and few negatives. Of course, this is nonsense, at least for the members of the Class of '74. Tragedy has spared none of them. Death, divorce, illness, and great stress are commonplace. One Class member had his house burn down. Another was shot while duck hunting. Some have gone through the trauma of trying (and failing) to conceive children. One has had a series of debilitating illnesses, and another lost his wife (and mother of three young children) to cancer. Spouses have walked out on a few. Children have rebelled. Close friends have suffered.

Again, what is interesting about the most successful members of this class is their capacity to turn terrible events—even their personal and family troubles—into growth experiences that make them stronger and more able. By not running away from tough times, and by reflecting seriously on their experiences, they grow. That growth, in turn, helps them to succeed.

But why don't all people behave this way? Many factors are probably involved, but one stands out to me. Low standards, a weak drive, and a lack of self-confidence in competitive situations undermine lifelong learning (see Exhibit 9.2). Without ambition, the pain of growth can simply look too big. Absent real drive, the budding entrepreneur never gets out of the corporate womb, the

### EXHIBIT 9.2

### How Competitive Drive and Lifelong Learning Contribute to Professional Success

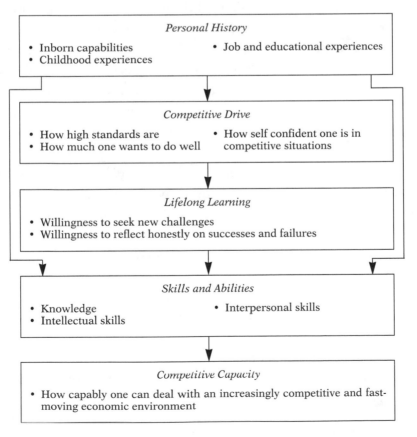

young consultant does not put up with the rejection that typically accompanies learning to successfully sell his or her services, the individual with leadership potential never takes the risk of trying to lead, and the junior deal maker never goes for the big deal where (win or lose) so much can be learned. Without real ambition, painful episodes from which one can learn so much are avoided both on and off the job. And with avoidance comes stagnation.

---

One of the most common complaints from the Class of '74 is that they have not had enough time to cope comfortably with all the demands placed on them. One of the reasons for the time pressures is the turbulent Phase III environment and the continuing education it demands. In a static world, one can invest little or no time in professional growth and do well. In today's non-static economy, little investment in growth ultimately derails success.

The 115 MBAs have mostly used four strategies for buying the extra time needed for learning. Some delayed marriage and family. Some gave virtually all family duties to their spouses. Some used money liberally to purchase personal support services. And many have turned time invested in family into a source of professional growth.

David Webber (Chapter 8), Stan Roberts (Chapter 7), Jeremy King (Chapter 2), and others delayed marriage and children until their late 20s or their 30s. Without family obligations, they focused on their jobs, including the huge learning challenge at work. Most seem to have recognized that this strategy had risks, that later in life they might have more difficulty finding a spouse or having children. But they chose to take those risks.

Some among the 115 found additional time by asking their spouses to handle all family activities. For the men, this was an extreme version of a traditional marriage, one that has been very difficult to maintain these days for many reasons. None of the women in the group had even the option of using this strategy.

A number of the class members have tried to buy their way out of the time problem. They have hired nannies, baby sitters, gardeners, tax accountants, even shoppers.* The costs involved can make this a very expensive undertaking. Nevertheless, some of the 115 clearly view this as an exceptionally wise investment.

Finally, many of those in the class have turned personal and family problems not only into a source of personal growth, but also into professionally relevant growth. Like David DeLong, they have transformed crises in their marriages, health problems, and clashes with children into important learnings that are also applicable on the job.

All four of these strategies have helped them manage their work-family relationships and helped them grow. And even a slight edge in growth can sometimes pay off big.

Imagine, for example, two people who are completely equal in terms of competitive capacity at age twenty-five. Both have, say, 100 units of talent. But the two have different orientations to life-long learning. One aggressively seeks challenges, reflects seriously on successes and failures, and grows. The other is somewhat less assertive in this regard. The interesting question is: how much will this single difference influence their capacity to compete in a Phase III environment? The answer is: much more than one might expect, because of the compounding effect.

For example: if the less aggressive learner grows at 4% per year, by the time he or she is fifty, the 100 units of talent will have grown to 256. In other words, this person will be able to cope with professional challenges that are more than twice as difficult as those he or she was able to handle at age twenty-five. But if the more aggressive learner grows at 9% per year, this individual at age fifty will have transferred 100 units of talent into 862. The better learner will be able to tackle tasks that are not twice but eight times as difficult as those performed at age twenty-five. As a re-

---

*Shoppers are people who, for a fee, do shopping for a client.

sult, two people who were clearly peers at one time are no longer in the same league. One can deal with problems at work that are over three times as difficult as the other (862/256 = 3.4). And this is far from an extreme example (see The Compounding Effect below).

In a Phase II type of economic environment, this differential in competitive capacity would not translate into a gigantic gap in incomes. The lack of global markets, barriers to competition among

---

### THE COMPOUNDING EFFECT

#### Case I

Both Fred and George have 100 units of relevant talent (or capacity) at age 25. Fred then grows at 9% per year while George grows at 4% per year. Net result at age 50:

$$\text{Fred has 862 units} \atop \text{George has 256 units} \quad > \quad {3.4 \atop 1}$$

#### Case II

In this scenario, Fred grows at 12% per year while George grows at 3% per year. Net result at age 50:

$$\text{Fred has 1862 units} \atop \text{George has 209 units} \quad > \quad {8.9 \atop 1}$$

#### Case III

In this scenario, Fred grows at 15% a year while George grows at 3%, and in addition, a changing environment means that 3% of their competitive capacities becomes obsolete each year. Net result, again at age 50:

$$\text{Fred has 1821 units} \atop \text{George has 100 units} \quad > \quad {18.2 \atop 1}$$

firms and inside firms, massive governmental income redistribu-
tions, and many other factors would have a leveling effect. But
Phase II is not today's reality. Today, differences in competitive capacity are turning into big differences in income—and lifelong
learning has become a major ingredient in stories of economic
success.

---

### NEW RULE #8

In a rapidly changing and competitive environment, formal
K-12-university education is very important, but insufficient.
Success at work demands huge growth after a terminal degree
to learn new approaches, skills, techniques, and more. A turbulent environment offers many opportunities for growth for
those willing to take some risks and to reflect honestly on their
experiences.

# PART IV

## IMPLICATIONS

# 10

## SUCCESS AT WORK

WHEN ASKED IN 1992 WHAT THEY WOULD BE DOING IN TEN YEARS, the 115 MBAs from the Class of '74 offered a variety of responses. Nearly 25% are still dreaming of becoming entrepreneurs of some sort. Another 20% to 25% think they will be out of the business world by then and into government, politics, teaching, or retirement. Still another 20% say they will be doing something different, although they are not sure exactly what. Few view their work in stable terms—same career, same job, same challenges, same income.

This outlook is partially a result of their highly motivated natures, although twenty years of successes and failures have clearly moderated their ambitions. As is typical of people when they grow older, the level of hunger- and career-oriented aggressiveness seems lower for this group in 1993 than it was in 1974.[1] For most of them, their implicit definition of a successful life has broadened. Within that, work appears to take less priority now relative to family commitments and personal health.[2] But even in that reduced state, career focus is high for these people compared to many in their generation.*

Their orientation to the future is also somewhat driven by the same kinds of dissatisfactions felt by other baby boomers. Although the 115 have been much more economically successful than average, expectations established in the 1950s and '60s have often not been fully met. Since their parents had a house nearly twice as big or luxurious as their grandparents', many expected a domicile twice as nice as mom's and dad's. With housing prices up tenfold over the last thirty years, with mortgage rates higher than their parents', and with their children's college educations costing five to ten times what they paid, expectations have sometimes been hard to meet even on $200,000 a year.

But most of all, their future outlook is driven by the same set of economic forces that have been so influential in shaping their careers thus far. These forces have created a business environment in which job opportunities in the United States are now found more often in smaller and more entrepreneurial settings; where consultants and others who aid big business are flourishing; where the rewards for being a good manager have decreased relative to the rewards for being a good leader, entrepreneur, or dealer; where the range of outcomes has grown, with the biggest incomes going to those with talent, education, motivation, and the willingness to take risks; where the kind of twenty year career plans once found in large firms are becoming museum pieces; and perhaps most fundamentally, where the very concept of careers is changing, and not just for MBAs.

Until recently, many moderately successful people at midlife looked to a static yet comfortable future at work. Careers were secure, but often boring. Over the last two decades, this arrangement has been changing. The patterns established in the middle of this century—go to school, get a job, progress, peak out, glide for decades into retirement—are being replaced by multiple careers,

---

*For example, they still work longer hours than most others their age.

lifelong learning, and a lot more uncertainty. In an increasingly competitive global marketplace, to stand still is to fall back. This new world can be more exciting and more personally fulfilling; it is for most of these MBAs. It can also be terrifying, especially for those without sufficient education, skills, and motivation.

———————

My study of 115 MBAs from the Class of '74 raises many questions, the most basic of which are these:

1. How have these people been so successful at work? In a tough economic environment, how have so many of them seemingly defied the laws of gravity?
2. Are their careers contributing to society? Are they adding sufficient value relative to their incomes?
3. Is it possible for more people to attain economic success and personal satisfaction at work despite the economic environment? If so, how?

Regarding the first set of questions, success for the 115 seems to be most directly related to the business context in which they have been working and to their ability to take advantage of that context. This environment has been increasingly fast moving and volatile, the product of numerous forces, the most important of which is globalization. A globalized economy has been offering more opportunities, often in the form of larger markets. But that same economy has also been creating more hazards, usually from increased competition.

To capitalize on the opportunities available to them while avoiding the hazards, these MBAs have drawn heavily upon high standards, a strong desire to win, and a willingness to grow and learn new abilities. These characteristics have helped them to develop a strong competitive capacity and to buck convention and try approaches to work that were different from mid-20th century norms. This has meant being more entrepreneurial and less bureaucratic. This has meant more leadership relative to management. It has meant a greater role for network-like relationships and a lesser role for hierarchy. It has meant financing for growth or renewal, not just business as usual. It has also required more risk taking and more volatile career paths (see Exhibit 10.1).

The least successful in the class have followed the guidelines in Exhibit 10.1 least closely. For a variety of reasons, their goals have been lower, their desire to win less. They have not been willing to buck convention as much as the others or to put themselves as much into challenging situations where they can grow. They have also been much more likely to end up in larger and more bureaucratic organizations, where they have managed routine through hierarchial relationships.

As a result of their capacity to adapt to the needs of the current economic environment, most of the 115 MBAs have clearly done very well for themselves. But how much of their activity has benefited others? Over the past decade, serious questions have been raised about the self-centeredness and greed of baby boomers in general, and MBAs from elite schools in particular. Some people have suggested that these individuals are as much a national liability as an asset. What do Class of '74 experiences tell us about these issues?

The extreme argument is hard to take seriously in light of their correspondence over the past two decades. Asked about important events in their lives, they write about marriages, births, and many items like these: "Over the last fourteen months, my team has successfully implemented a new quality process at our facilities here and in Europe (1983)." "When I came into the job, the division was losing over $500,000 a month and major layoffs were imminent. Today, we are making over a million a month and we have actually started hiring again (1989)." "I have helped my number one client experience a turnaround that has increased its market value by over $1 billion and has improved significantly its products and services (1986)." "My little investment bank, now eight years old, has successfully helped over fifty important clients and has developed a reputation as the premier firm in its line of business

EXHIBIT 10.1

THE NEW RULES

### New Realities

Do not rely on convention; career paths that were winners for most of this century are often no longer providing much success.

Keep your eyes on globalization and its consequences; everything is changing, offering both gigantic new opportunities and equally large hazards.

### New Responses

Move toward the small and entreprenurial and away from the big and bureaucratic; speed and flexibility are winning in an increasingly competitive world.

Help big business from the oustide as well as on the inside; huge opportunities exist for consultants and other service providers.

Do not just manage; now you must also lead to help make organizations winners.

Wheel and deal if you can; huge opportunities exist in financial and other deal maker careers.

### Underpinnings

Increase your competitive drive; high standards and a desire to win are essential today and in the future.

Never stop trying to grow; lifelong learning is increasingly necessary for success.

(1991)." "As director of marketing, I was responsible for the most successful product launched in the company's history—over $75 million in sales (1982)." "I was sent to Korea to help set up a joint venture. Despite many problems associated with having two different companies, two different national cultures, and so forth, we have created an organization that is producing innovative technology and is making money (1987)." "My own company, now ten years old, has served many thousands of customers with a unique product. There is pride in this (1992)." Even if one discounts these assertions by some hubris factor, the accomplishments are still very real and socially useful. These MBAs have been starting businesses, building businesses, and turning around businesses. They have been funding entrepreneurs and growing organizations. They have been employing people, paying taxes, and producing useful products and services. They have been supplying needed leadership to economic organizations. Without all these activities, the tough economy we have witnessed over the past two decades would undoubtedly have been worse. Perhaps much worse. "The MBAs are EVIL" argument just does not fit the facts.

The question of whether their contributions are adequate, or are as high as they should be given their incomes, is far more complicated. A few of them are probably paid salaries that are totally out of proportion to any rational measure of contribution. But critics of business incomes point most often to the case of CEOs of big companies who induce complacent boards into ridiculous compensation packages.[3] This criticism is valid.[4] Of the many very successful people in the Class of '74, the number who fit that description today—big company CEOs, controlled boards, bloated compensation packages—is zero. Not few, zero. And the number that could become such people in the next two decades is very small because the vast majority are pursuing other career paths.

Most of those in the class are now talking about how they hope to make a bigger social contribution over the next two decades. For some, the idea is charitable work, for others, government service or simply using their influence to run economic organizations to benefit as many people as possible. If they achieve their aspirations in this regard, I think it will be very difficult in 2014 to criticize their success. If they fall far short of their aspirations, some social critics will probably conclude that they were greedy or irresponsible. If I had to place a bet today, I would lean toward the more optimistic scenario—in which they increasingly give more and more back to society.

---

Is it possible to help more people to succeed like the Class of '74? Because these individuals have had the advantage of a Harvard MBA on their résumés, it is tempting to say no or to be pessimistic. But my own experiences over the last two decades lead me to reject that idea. We should never underestimate the power of the privileges that many of these MBAs have had. Nevertheless, I have seen dozens of other individuals, most of them without MBA degrees, approach work and career in ways similar to the Class of '74 and then succeed greatly, at least by most standards. They have simply acted in accordance with the implications of Exhibit 10.1. Those implications are many and powerful. And they are just as relevant to the Class of '94 as they have been to the Class of '74.

In regard to careers, especially managerial careers, implications include these:

1. Settling for good, much less mediocrity, is dangerous. In an increasingly competitive environment, the person or organization that has a goal of being #1 or #2 will always beat an equally talented individual or group that is content with just doing well. This may sound obvious, yet the reality is that the vast majority of the workforce does not manage careers today according to this principle. Large numbers of people have been taught by big business, big labor, and big government that fair-to-good is adequate. This may have been true in certain places twenty years ago; ten years from now fair-to-good will probably NEVER lead to success.

2. Becoming excellent at some activity requires a careful matching of individual strengths and weaknesses with the opportunities that are available. This fitting of capabilities to context demands,

above all, self-awareness. The organization-man of the 1950s had no idea who he really was, yet he could still succeed by conforming to a slow-moving environment. That career strategy does not work in a rapidly changing world. Furthermore, in a dynamic context, an honest and realistic assessment of oneself is also essential for efficient growth. Since people cannot grow on all dimensions all the time, they need to know where there are important gaps between future challenges and present capabilities—an assessment which is impossible without self-awareness.

3. To develop needed skills and attitudes, it is increasingly important to get a good education, where "good" means an environment in which standards are high, where self-confidence in competitive situations is built, and where people learn to want to learn more. Conversely, it is wise to avoid educational institutions where standards are low and where students are alienated from learning. Again, this may sound obvious, but stop and consider: are all the students you know (yourself, your children, your friends, etc.) really in institutions that meet this standard? Think about it.

4. After college, anyone who is ambitious should pause before joining a traditional 20th century corporation. These big and bureaucratic firms not only offer fewer opportunities than they did twenty years ago, they also sometimes have environments that are not conducive to growth and lifelong learning. There are exceptions, of course, but the days are long gone when it was rational to jump at a job offer from a large, well-known firm.

5. Ambitious people should also probably avoid industries that are less competitive than the world norm. An industry with a low level of competitiveness can be a sanctuary from tough times for a while, but never long term. Even monopoly environments like electric utilities are moving into much more competitive futures. The risk one takes by working in such a setting, especially early in a career, is that lessons and skills that will be needed in the future are simply not learned.

6. Vertical movement up a single functional hierarchy makes much less sense today than it did for most of this century. Although such a career can give the illusion of success, at least for a

while, it does not provide the breadth needed to cope with a fast moving and competitive world. Today, it is probably better to seek more non-linear paths in which more can be learned.

7. To facilitate lifelong learning, people need to look for positions that are a stretch, bosses who encourage subordinate growth, and environments that allow for some experimentation and innovation. A successful career may increasingly mean avoiding jobs with little growth potential and companies that do not want their employees to grow. Increasingly, bureaucratic and risk-averse environments are career killers because of their impact on learning.

8. A drive for success has probably always involved certain hazards. But ethical traps are more common now than a generation ago. In a volatile world, it is easy to step over moral boundaries. This is especially true where big money is at stake. Ethical judgment is increasingly important.

9. For those who have not been fortunate enough to have great parents and a great education, the lessons in Exhibit 10.1 are especially important. The business environment is not going to get easier. Just the opposite is true.

Each of these points raises additional issues and questions that nearly everyone would be well advised to consider—for themselves, their children, their spouses, fellow employees, and friends. Perhaps the most fundamental issue is this: anyone who is in an environment that is not helping prepare him or her for an even tougher Phase III future should move out of that environment as fast as possible. AS FAST AS POSSIBLE.

---

Bigness, in the form of business, labor, and government, is all too often out of touch with the times. Some of these institutions are still behaving as if we were living in a Phase II economy. The net result: big corporations are shrinking in size, big labor is losing market share, and big government has less and less respect from voters.

The story of the Class of '74 suggests some important implications for those trying to successfully run large organizations:

1. The number one managerial objective in most big firms should be creating a revolution. Unlike a half century ago, traditional corporations are no longer in a strongly advantaged position. The dinosaur image is not a bad one. In today's post-corporate world, unless managers can genetically reengineer these firms, they will disappear.

2. The goal of the revolution should be to become much less hierarchial, bureaucratic, inwardly focused, and political. The objective is to move from a tall hierarchy focus to a flexible network organization. This goal will require restructuring, cost cutting, and process engineering. But most fundamentally, it will require cultural change.

3. Another way to think about this: the goal of a big business person should be to create an organization that feels and operates like a smaller business, yet retains the resource advantages of bigness. This means operating with speed and simplicity, having employees feel a sense of ownership, and orienting everyone to the customer. Doing this in most large organizations requires significant cultural change.

4. Cultural change in larger and older organizations is enormously difficult. Without strong leadership from many people, including some at the very top of the organization, such change is probably impossible.

5. Big business executives who think their cultures and organizations are fine should answer the following question: How many of the best university graduates did you attract last year? If the answer is zero, or close to zero, the culture may still be a serious problem.

6. The number one impediment to cultural change in large organizations is a lack of urgency fostered by too much historical success and not enough bold leadership. In most big businesses today, it is essential to increase the urgency level.

7. Managers in large governmental organizations face especially difficult challenges, but ones that are not impossible. A catalog of recent public sector success stories shows a trend that looks very similar to what is happening in the private sector.[5] Organizations are slimming down, reducing layers, becoming more externally focused, and forming tighter relationships with suppliers and customers. All this is happening at a snail's pace for dozens of reasons, not the least of which is the mind-set coming from our political parties.* The process needs to be pushed faster.

8. Anyone in a large organization who thinks major change is impossible should probably get out. Sitting inside a big firm and pretending that it is 1955 is crazy, even if one has a "good" job in a "good" company. It is better to go to another big organization where change is possible or go to a small firm and help reinvent large companies from the outside-in.

---

As I write this in late 1993, there is a growing pessimism about managerial careers. The number of individuals taking the Graduate Management Admissions Test in the United States has dropped off after decades of growth. Middle level managers in many businesses say that there are too many managers and not enough jobs. As long as one thinks about managerial careers with a mid-twentieth century mind-set, this pessimism is perfectly logical. But if one recognizes what is happening in the business world today, how so

---

*Too many people in one of the parties seem to think that we still live in a Phase II world, and that, if anything, government organizations need only to grow still bigger in order to serve society well. The other party sometimes seems to behave as if we were back in Phase I, a century ago, and to think that governmental structures simply need to shrink back to an 1890's size. Neither of these perspectives recognizes that a Phase III world places very different demands on organizations, both public and private, than did earlier eras.

much is changing, and the tremendous opportunities created by this change, the rationale that leads to pessimism largely disappears.

For the foreseeable future, a globalizing economy will offer many, many opportunities for nearly everyone, even those (women and non-whites) who saw limited options in management over the last century.*[6] Such is the nature of change; it tends to shake up established power structures.

I am even cautiously optimistic about big businesses. Leadership is emerging in some large firms, creating revolutions, and thus developing powerful competitive capabilities. This is not happening as fast as it should, or as pervasively, but it is happening. And on average, this seems to be happening more in big businesses centered in the United States than in large firms in most of the rest of the world, probably because the United States is further into a Phase III-like environment than are most other countries.

If we have anything to worry about legitimately, it is less the opportunities than our capacity to equip people to take advantage of these opportunities. Here I think we are vulnerable, which is why I have chosen to end this book on the topic of education.

---

*This has been the recent pattern in entrepreneurship. The number of businesses owned by women increased by 57% in the late 1980s. Those owned by Hispanics rose 81%, by blacks 38%.[6]

# 11

---

# EDUCATION FOR THE
# 21ST CENTURY

---

THE U.S. LABOR FORCE IN 1993 IS MADE UP OF ABOUT 120 MILLION people.[1] The average daily wage for those in manufacturing has been around $92.00. In service industries, salaries are usually lower. These wages appear to be unacceptable to the majority of baby boomers. Like our Class of '74 MBAs, they were taught to expect to live better than their parents, just as their fathers and mothers had lived better than their parents. Most cannot live up to this expectation on $20,000 to $25,000 a year.

Wage growth in the United States has been stalled for twenty years by a variety of factors associated with the globalization of the economy. Unlike thirty or forty or fifty years ago, people in manufacturing face real competition from those in the European community, who on average earn somewhat less, those in Japan, who are often more productive, those in Taiwan, Hong Kong, Korea, Malaysia, and Singapore, who earn less than half the U.S. wage, and increasingly those in Mexico, who earn about $10 a day ($2,500 per year). Even in some manufacturing industries that are not global in any sense, wages are being retarded because those firms sell to other businesses that are facing international competition and that are in turn demanding lower costs from suppliers.

The same global forces that are holding down manufacturing wages in the United States are indirectly hurting salaries in service industries. Sometimes this is because out-of-work production workers are seeking employment in services, pushing wage levels down. Sometimes this is because manufacturing firms are being forced to seek cheaper and cheaper suppliers of services. Sometimes this is because flat wages in manufacturing are forcing people to search for less expensive personal services.

As difficult as this situation is now from the point of view of an American worker, it may become much worse. When I have asked the Class of '74, almost all have predicted that a Phase III economic era is far from over. Most seem to believe that competitive pressures will continue to increase over the next decade, with Eastern Europe and the former USSR trying desperately to solve their economic and social problems by competing successfully against firms in the United States. The workforce in those countries is nearly twice the size of ours, is often well educated, and currently has an average manufacturing wage of about $7 or $8 a day ($2,000 per year). But even this threat is dwarfed by the less developed parts of Asia. In China, India, Pakistan, Indonesia, Vietnam, and Thailand, there is a potential labor force of nearly a billion people and a current manufacturing wage of about $2 a day ($500 per year). Until recently, people in China or even Hungary would not have been able to compete against those in the United States because of lack of capital, management expertise, workforce skills, or political support. But this is changing rapidly.

Many factors can slow this trend. Political instability in low-wage countries will keep out needed capital and expertise. Political pressures in the United States will try to enact policy and legislation to stall the inevitable.* But overlying all this are very

---

*This can be clearly seen in the 1993 debate on the North American Free Trade Agreement (NAFTA).

powerful economic forces, including the natural desire of virtually all of humanity to improve their physical conditions.

Coping with this reality will require a multitude of changes.[2] U.S. corporations are going to have to take many more steps to make them competitive against the best from outside of America. Despite progress made in the last decade, far too many medium and large firms are still too bureaucratic and inwardly focused. U.S. financial and regulatory systems still provide too many incentives for socially useless activity and too few incentives for behaviors we need.* And the U.S. labor force still needs to significantly increase its capabilities, especially at the low end.

The qualities that virtually all Americans need to succeed today, and will need to succeed in the foreseeable future, are aptly demonstrated by the Class of '74. Motivation, self-confidence, and a willingness to take risks are essential. So is a good education[†] and a dedication to further growth throughout one's life.

It is very difficult to imagine how the United States can prosper and fulfill a useful global role unless it witnesses a dramatic improvement in the education, skills, and motivation of its labor force. A poorly skilled workforce will increasingly result in direct competition with those in developing nations, a prospect that seems fair neither to those countries nor to unskilled workers in the United States. An acceptable future, to Americans and others, would probably have our labor force playing a high-end-niche role. In such a vision, we would allow low-skilled manufacturing jobs to continue to move offshore while we concentrate on those

---

*Lester Thurow puts it this way: "The entire regulatory framework governing finance and industry must be altered so that the biggest profits and highest incomes are paid to those who expand production and output rather than to those who rejiggle financial assets."[3]

[†]People without a high school diploma earn, on average, less than $10,000 per year, a salary that is acceptable to very few people in the United States today. People with only a high school education earn less than $15,000 per year, again a salary that satisfies few.[4]

higher-skilled jobs which can meet the average American's economic expectations.

Creating a top-of-the-line workforce will require an educational and training system that is far better than that which exists today. Is top-of-the-line consistent with a current high school dropout rate close to 30%, nearly five times higher than Japan's?[5] Is it consistent with the fact that 17% of American seventeen-year-olds are said to be functionally illiterate?[6] Is it consistent with the skill levels of those who do graduate from high school and from many colleges? Or the lack of science and math education?[7] Or the lack of training in general for the majority of the workforce after they leave school?

For at least a decade now, experts have been telling us that to prosper in the future we need to make much better use of our human resources. This means not allowing people to stop growing at age ten or twenty or thirty. It means pushing skill growth rates up rather than allowing children and adults to coast and stagnate. Although following this advice is not easy, we should keep the following in mind. If we do not go this route, vast numbers of Americans may do poorly in a global labor market, while a few people will do exceptionally well. As a result, the gap between the rich and poor in the United States will grow and grow—until something explodes.*

---

Members of the Class of '74 were in elementary and secondary schools in the 1950s and 1960s. Few attended elite private institutions. Nevertheless, most were served reasonably well by their schools for at least two reasons. The most obvious relates

---

*In a sense, this was how Phase I of big business capitalism ended—with the roaring '20s and a stock market crash.

to the lack of the severe behavioral problems one sometimes finds today. None of the 115 entered school through metal detectors. None mourned the death of classmates by violence or drugs. But the more important reason that they were served well was because the educational system was often designed for people like themselves—individuals who were reasonably smart and very motivated to perform in school. While they were growing up, the emphasis in class, in sports, and elsewhere was on preparing people with talent and drive to go to the best university possible. The United States had made a special commitment to college education with the G.I. bill. As more and more universities were built, and as older schools expanded, elementary and secondary teachers were expected to fill those seats. Even the Russians helped. Sputnik encouraged President Eisenhower and Congress to pass the National Defense Education Act. That legislation provided extra funding for science and math training. The money was spent on physics and calculus classes for the best students. No funding was allocated to train the future manufacturing worker in the elementary statistical skills he or she would someday need to compete with the Japanese.

Since the Class of '74 left high school, early education has in most cases gotten worse, especially relative to other industrial countries.* Over the last decade, report after report has provided depressing statistics and conclusions about the status of elementary and secondary education in the United States.[9] During this same period, there have been some improvements, but they have come only sporadically and slowly.[10] Rarely do we hear about the successful implementation of higher standards. Rarely do we hear

---

*In their award-winning book, Ray Marshall and Mark Tucker summarize the facts by saying, "Whether one judges by comparison to the performance of other countries or by comparison to the demands of the workplace, school graduates fall far short of what is needed and what others have achieved."[8]

that children are graduating with more self-confidence in competitive situations. Rarely do we hear that students are learning to love learning and to understand its future importance throughout their lifetimes.

At one level, the issue is simple. The world is different today than it was thirty years ago and schools need to adapt. But they are either not adapting or are doing so much too slowly. In this sense, they are behaving like large industrial companies when the economic environment shifted from Phase II to Phase III.

It is tempting when analyzing this issue, or any problem for that matter, to look for people to blame. In elementary and secondary education, there is no shortage of potential villains: teachers' unions, teachers, educational bureaucrats, left-wing interest groups, right-wing interest groups, apathetic parents, parochial politicians, stingy or short-sighted communities. This manner of thinking is useless, even dangerous. If ever there was a systems or culture problem that transcends specific individuals or groups, we have it in K-12 education.

Ironically, the heart of the problem is related to too much success. Imagine a company with total revenues of $6.25 billion in 1950 that today has sales of more than $250 billion per year, roughly four times as big as IBM. This firm would be the largest corporation on earth. Because it has experienced more success (in terms of growth) than General Motors, IBM, or Sears, one might expect it to have certain problems on an even bigger scale than those three industry leaders—problems associated with too much success and the arrogant, internally focused, bureaucratic, and political cultures that often come with growth. The firm in this case is Elementary and Secondary Education Inc.[11] And the cultural problems are indeed mammoth.

The lessons the Class of '74 learned about turning around corporations with unadaptive cultures may be relevant here. Those lessons are: 1) Dealing with these situations is a phenomenally difficult task. Initial proclamations of what will be required are usually totally inadequate. 2) A severe crisis is often needed. In business, that is typically created by strong competition. 3) Crisis or not, especially capable leadership is needed, leadership that is not wedded to the status quo.

If corporate experiences are relevant,* I would predict the following.[13] In the absence of real competition, crisis, and bold leadership, we will have more or less the same problems ten years from now that we have today. A few hundred more reports will be written, but they will have had little real impact. The GM/Sears/IBM experiences tell us that people in positions of power in school systems will find dozens of ways to show that criticisms are overstated, that they are making adequate improvements, or that the problems are beyond their control (i.e. too little funding, too many poorly motivated students, etc.).

Members of the Class of '74 are very concerned about this problem. They are concerned as employers, as citizens, and as parents. Many are frustrated that they cannot do more to help deal with these issues. And some are becoming increasingly cynical about the seeming ineffectiveness of the political process in solving educational problems.

A comparison with higher education is relevant here. Although U.S. colleges and universities have difficulties too, virtually everyone seems to agree that they are in vastly better shape than elementary and secondary schools.[14] Both have huge numbers of students, served at thousands of locations, and both have experienced much growth over the last century. Defenders of secondary and elementary education argue that higher education has a much easier task. This may or may not be true. What is unquestionably true is the following: the percentage of schools in higher education that have a monopoly is zero while the percentage of lower level

---

*In their book *Thinking for a Living: Education and the Wealth of Nations*, former U.S. Labor Secretary Ray Marshall and Mark Tucker say, "The lessons our best firms have learned, we believe, hold the key to great advances in schools."[12] I agree.

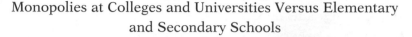

EXHIBIT 11.1

Monopolies at Colleges and Universities Versus Elementary
and Secondary Schools

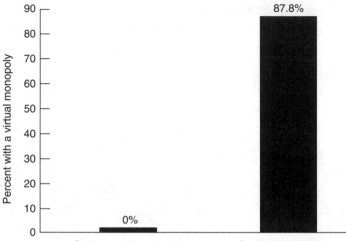

*Data adapted from *Statistical Abstract of US 1992*, Page 138, Table
210

schools with a virtual monopoly is about 88%. Corporate experiences tell us this single difference can have an overwhelmingly
powerful effect when it comes to adaptation and change.

Because I am not an expert in elementary and secondary education, I am not in a position to evaluate the many proposals for reform which are now being advanced. But after watching the Class
of '74 for twenty years, one conclusion is very clear to me. Unless
we can improve early education, significant numbers of people
over the next few decades are going to find it very difficult to
achieve even a modest degree of success at work. Unless we can
help schools to increase students' competitive drive and desire for
lifelong learning, we are all going to suffer the consequences. And
that includes every single businessman and -woman operating in
the United States.

Because higher education in the United States is in so much better shape than elementary and secondary, it is tempting to withhold criticism of universities. But that is surely a mistake. Colleges also sometimes undermine our capacity to compete in a Phase III economy, and probably for the same fundamental reason found in K-12 education—too much success. Total revenues for colleges and universities have gone from about $1 billion in 1946 to nearly $164 billion in 1991.[15] As a result, even with competition that has forced some change, one can still find some lack of external focus in higher education too. Universities can easily get onto tracks that look bizarre to outsiders. Sometimes these activities are creative and appropriate; sometimes they are simply out of touch with the needs of society.

Business programs are an especially relevant example here. Critics have been arguing for at least fifteen years that business schools are not always producing the kind of product that the U.S. economy needs.[16] According to this perspective, too many graduates do not have the interpersonal, leadership, and teamwork skills that are necessary to help make firms more competitive. They are also said to lack the international perspective needed in a Phase III economy. They are criticized for being too arrogant, self-centered, and willing to pursue money-making ventures that contribute little to society. If business schools were closely in touch with the career experiences of their alumni, they would see that these criticisms have some validity. But many schools are not as familiar with alumni careers as they should be because they are too inwardly focused. This lack of external orientation has numerous roots, but much is related to success. Business school revenues have grown astronomically over the past thirty to forty years. In 1960, there were fewer than 75,000 people with MBA degrees working anywhere on earth. Today that figure exceeds 1,250,000. In 1960, about 52,000 people received undergraduate degrees in business management from U.S. universities. In 1990, nearly a quarter of a million people received those degrees. Since 1979, the most popular undergraduate degree granted in the United States has been in business management.[17]

Class of '74 experiences suggest that MBA programs, and probably most of higher education, face major adaptation challenges in an increasingly fast-moving world. If ever there was a time for schools to stop and address fundamental questions, it is now. The most important issues are probably the most basic. What role can and should higher education play today? Colleges and universities that are inwardly focused on their faculties have a tendency to think of their mission in terms of teaching specific areas of knowledge. This is especially true at research-oriented institutions. But in the case of the Class of '74, we find that Harvard sometimes missed the boat on specific knowledge areas: too little was taught about situations outside the United States, about small business and entrepreneurship, about what was wrong with big business, and about the difference between management and leadership. Yet despite this, the 115 have done remarkably well. This means either that Harvard Business School was irrelevant, or that it was a minor liability, or that the contributions it made were mostly not in terms of simple knowledge transfer. When I have asked the Class of '74 about this, they have always chosen the third alternative, stressing how the School helped develop analytical and problem-solving skills, bolstered self-confidence, gave access to certain jobs and companies,* and facilitated the development of a network of friendships and contacts.

Perhaps the most fundamental issue here relates to the very concept of what education is. For decades, formal schooling has been conceived as something one provides the young to prepare them for work and life. The least capable get a terminal degree in high school. Others get their final degrees in college or graduate school. Then they go work and live; learning is over. The world of

---

*Another criticism of prestigious business schools is that they are simply expensive employment agencies. Most members of the Class of '74 agree that HBS served a placement/recruiting function, but say that that was only one of many benefits.

the early 21st century will be one in which learning must go on, out of necessity, throughout working life. In a Phase III economy, increasing levels of competition create more and more change. The person who attempts to coast, only applying what he or she has learned in the past, will have an increasingly difficult time being competitive in a tough global labor market. Economic forces will make the maxim GROW OR DIE.

Adapting to this new reality is not easy. The whole concept of lifelong learning challenges core ideas about education. Why, for example, should business schools offer a two year "terminal" degree to people at age twenty-five? Why not a one year program at twenty-five and a month long program at twenty-eight, thirty-one, thirty-four, and so forth? Or to reduce the clear demarcation between school and work, perhaps MBA programs should not be conducted on campuses and in classrooms. Technological change certainly is offering more and more possibilities here.

Class of '74 experiences suggest that a major issue for all educators is to help students desire to learn more, learn how to learn, and thus be able to adapt to changing circumstances. I think Harvard did that back in 1972 and 1973, at least to some degree, by making the program very challenging. The School showed the 115 future MBAs how much could be learned when they got out of their comfort zones into a tough (but not impossible) experience, took some risks, and then reflected on the results. By doing this, the program not only stretched them at the time, it also made difficult circumstances less frightening, thus increasing the chances that they would seek big challenges in their future jobs and continue to grow.*

For decades, visionary educators have been advocating university programs that go beyond simple knowledge transfer, that

---

*As I write this in late 1993, Harvard Business School is undertaking the largest ever reassessment of its MBA program. Based on what I have learned as a result of this examination, I am not sure that the School is doing as good a job of challenging students in 1993 as it did in 1974. I hope we will remedy this situation with the changes that are being recommended as a result of that reassessment.

focus on skills and values that will help people even when specific knowledge becomes outdated. Unfortunately, too many schools have embraced these ideas more in their rhetoric than in reality. To help their graduates succeed at work in the 21st century, this must change.

---

With the growth of higher education over the past fifty years, a few dozen top schools have found that they have so many applications that they can be extremely selective. Only one person in six is accepted by Harvard Business School today. Very high ratios of applications to admissions can also be found at a number of colleges and at the best graduate schools in law, medicine, and business. To make it into Yale Law School or Stanford Medical School today, one has to jump hundreds of hurdles starting relatively early in life. As a consequence, these schools are not only getting very talented students, they are also, like HBS, getting extremely competitive individuals. From Class of '74 experiences, I would conclude that a key reason that alumni from these schools do well in their careers is because the admission process brings in people with high standards and a strong desire to win.

The very competitive individuals now attending universities have sometimes grown up without much institutionalized religion, within "value free" schools, and with absentee parents—certainly more so than the Class of '74. When today's students graduate, they are going into a world that is faster moving and with less regulation than existed in most of this century. Highly competitive individuals, sometimes weak moral compasses, and a wide open business environment all combine in a potentially explosive way.

For over a decade now, some people have been urging business, law, and medical schools to deal with this "ethics" issue.* For the

---

*At Harvard, for example, this challenge came from former President Derek Bok.

most part, schools have resisted. Some have argued that one cannot teach values to twenty-five year olds. Others say that pushing one set of ideals is not appropriate in a multicultural world. There is some truth in both arguments. But there is a great deal of defensiveness too.

Whether they intend to or not, schools always teach value lessons. In management education, each and every day students are given cases or readings and then directed by instructors to focus on the specific issues in which those faculty members specialize. Sometimes there are broader, bigger, moral issues lurking in the background, but more often than not the specialist faculty ignore them, and thus direct students to ignore them, because they are tangential to the subject matter in the course. This process can inadvertently signal to students that it is acceptable to walk through life with blinders, focusing only on matters in which one has expertise while ignoring the broader consequences.

Business schools clearly need to spend more time talking about the bigger and softer issues. For example: what is success at work? Most of those in the Class of '74 appear to equate this term with high income in a satisfying job which makes some social contribution and does not undermine one's family life. Does this definition stress income too much and other factors too little? Put another way, is the 3.05 average social contribution score from Chapter 7 as high as it should be? It is impossible to make a case that the typical person in the class is pursuing personal gain regardless of the consequences to others. Nevertheless, after reading a draft of this book, some of the 115 have said that they believe 3.05 is certainly too low and that MBA programs speak of success too much in economic terms.

The largest issue of all, regarding the purpose of enterprise itself, surely needs more discussion and analysis. Without that sense of broader purpose, highly competitive people are like unguided missiles—powerful and dazzling, but potentially very destructive.

The recent increase in the diversity of student bodies presents both problems and opportunities here. When upper-middle-class white men from the United States represented three quarters of the class at Harvard Business School and similar institutions, upper-middle-class white American male faculty could talk about values in an offhand way and experience few difficulties. Now that the student body (and to a much lesser degree, the faculty) includes a significant number of women, non-Americans, and non-whites, those same pronouncements can create misunderstandings and conflict. Under these circumstances, it is very tempting to retreat from any discussion of values. But the consequences of such a strategy are bad and will only grow worse in the future.

One opportunity presented by an increasingly diverse population at universities is to create a value message that makes sense for the 21st century. Diversity creates conflict, but it can also lead to innovation. If ever there was an area that needed creative thinking, it is the role of ethics training at colleges and universities.

For those who think this commentary is unfair—U.S. universities are acknowledged to be the best in the world—please consider the following. Higher education is no longer a small operation set in an ivory tower. Today it is a huge endeavor. For most of history, people in influential roles in business and elsewhere did not even have the equivalent of a modern high school education much less a graduate degree. That is rapidly changing.* As a society, we have placed a very large bet on the efficacy of university training—not as a vehicle for simple knowledge transfer, but as a force for making life better on earth. When higher education was a cottage industry, the mistakes it made had little impact. Mistakes today can have a giant influence on all of us.

Even those in the Class of '74, who for the most part are very satisfied with their MBA experience, believe universities and business schools can do better. Harry Turner speaks for many when he says: "Just as corporations are learning that they must constantly strive to improve, not become complacent, and adapt sensibly with the changes occurring around them, so must universities." This is

---

*An interesting example of this is the Clinton cabinet where sixteen of the first twenty cabinet level appointees had graduate degrees.[18]

probably true for the humblest little college, the big state university, and even for Harvard Business School.

Because graduates of HBS and some other fine schools have been so successful, it is enormously tempting to ignore Turner's advice. Let well enough alone. If it is not broken, etc. Employed for years at GM and IBM and Sears, that attitude is increasingly deadly. In a fast-moving and competitive world, past success does not ensure future success. Just the opposite, past success often makes it more difficult to succeed in the future. If ever there was a truth that we should all contemplate, this is one. And it applies equally to educational institutions, corporations, and individuals.

# ACKNOWLEDGMENTS

BETWEEN 1973 AND 1994, DOZENS OF INDIVIDUALS HAVE HELPED with this endeavor, including John Beck, Martha Beck, Andrew Burtis, Russ Eisenstat, Rob Friedman, Linda Hill, Jim Leahey, Nancy Rothbard, Nicki Steckler, and Mark Opel. One colleague, Jeff Sonnenfeld, played a central role for an entire decade. Larry Fouraker, John McArthur, Ray Corey, Jay Lorsch, Warren McFarlan, and Richard Rosenbloom all helped with the funding. In the preparation of this manuscript, many people have commented on early drafts, including Joe Badaracco, By Barnes, Warren Bennis, Mark Blankenship, Gail de Boissard, Jerome de Boissard, Richard Boyatzis, Jeff Bradach, Andrew Burtis, Tim Butler, Dan Casey, Nelson Chu, Jay Conger, Dwight Crane, Mariella Dearman, Nancy Dearman, Greg Dees, Barbara Devine, Bob Eccles, Russ Eisenstat, Bill Ellet, Alan Frohman, Jack Gabarro, David Garvin, Richard Hackman, Don Harris, Sam Hayes, Ellen Herman, Jim Heskett, Linda Hill, Hermi Ibarra, Rosabeth Kanter, John Kim, Bob Lambrix, Gina LaRoche, Paul Lawrence, Pat Light, Geoff Love, Gary Loveman, Jay Lorsch, Warren McFarlan, Quinn Mills, Sharon Parks, Krishna Palepu, Maury Peiperl, Rob Robinson, Nancy Rothbard, Mal Salter, Ed Schein, Virginia Smith, Scott Snook, Howard Stevenson, Richard Tedlow, David Thomas, Rick Walleigh, and David Wesley. Without all of their assistance, this book would not have been possible.

# NOTES

*Introduction*

1. These projects are reported more fully in *Power in Management* (NY: Amacom, 1979), and in five books published by The Free Press: *The General Managers* (1982), *Power and Influence: Beyond Formal Authority* (1985), *The Leadership Factor* (1988), *A Force for Change: How Leadership Differs from Management* (1990), and *Corporate Culture and Performance* (1992, with Jim Heskett).

2. Schein has reported results from that work in a number of places, most notably in *Career Dynamics*, Reading, Mass.: Addison-Wesley, 1978.

3. See *Adaptation to Life* by George Vaillant (Boston: Little, Brown and Co., 1977).

4. During the winter of 1973 and the spring of 1974, I talked to 150 Harvard MBA students about participating in a study of managerial careers. Half had been in an elective course entitled Self Assessment and Career Development. The rest had taken the entire required curriculum together as a group. All gave a preliminary commitment to fill out an annual questionnaire for at least five to ten years and to make themselves available for occasional interviews. Those who had taken the Self Assessment course also provided copies of the psychological tests and papers that they had generated as a part of their class work.

In January 1975, I mailed the first questionnaire. Another was sent in January 1976, a third and fourth in 1977 and 1978. 115 people replied to almost all of these inquiries, twenty-five individuals responded to none, and another ten returned one or two questionnaires but not the rest. By comparing the 115 on basic dimensions like age, grades, and socioeconomic status of parents to the overall Class of 1974, I found them to be similar, so I dropped the other thirty-five from the study. After persistent follow-up, over 90% of the remaining group responded to each subsequent mailing.

The questionnaires evolved over the years; the 1992 version is very different from the one in 1975. The average was eight pages long. Most of the surveys asked a wide variety of questions about jobs and satisfaction with different aspects of life. Almost all also included an open-ended question about key events in the prior twelve months. On three occasions, selected individuals were interviewed: thirty-seven in 1979, fifty-two in 1984, and eighty-three in 1991/92. These discussions were usually unstructured, lasted an hour and a half, and were conducted at the person's office or home.

*Chapter 1. Is the American Dream Dead?*

1. All names have been disguised.

2. From "The Fortune Directory, 1958," a supplement to the August 1958 *Fortune* magazine.

3. See the *1989 Fact Book on Higher Education* compiled by Deborah J. Carter and Andrew G. Malizio with Boichi San, American Council on Education, New York: Macmillan Publishing, 1989.

4. From *Fortune*, May 1974, Page 225.

5. See Ross Perot's *United We Stand: How We Can Take Back Our Country*, New York: Hyperion, 1992, Page 14.

6. See Page 101 in Frank S. Levy and Richard C. Michel, *The Economic Future of American Families: Income and Wealth Trends*, Washington, D.C.: Urban Institute Press, 1991.

7. Page 2 in *The New Individualists*, New York: Harper Collins, 1991.

8. Regarding time with first employer, as of 1992:

| Years | % of '74 Group | Years | % of '74 Group | Years | % of '74 Group |
|-------|----------------|-------|----------------|-------|----------------|
| 1 | 15% | 7 | 6% | 13 | 3% |
| 2 | 24% | 8 | 2% | 14 | 1% |
| 3 | 9% | 9 | 2% | 15 | 2% |
| 4 | 6% | 10 | 2% | 16 | 1% |
| 5 | 8% | 11 | 3% | 17 | 0% |
| 6 | 3% | 12 | 2% | 18 | 13% |

9. Regarding number of jobs '74–'92

| Number | % of Class | Number | % of Class | Number | % of Class |
|--------|-----------|--------|-----------|--------|-----------|
| 1 | 0% | 6 | 12% | 11 | 9% |
| 2 | 2% | 7 | 9% | 12 | 8% |
| 3 | 1% | 8 | 18% | 13 | 1% |
| 4 | 4% | 9 | 8% | 14 | 1% |
| 5 | 10% | 10 | 17% | 15 | 0% |

10. Regarding their job history:

| | 1975 | 1979 | 1984 | 1989 | 1992 |
|---|------|------|------|------|------|
| • Assistant to or Trainee | 27% | 0% | 0% | 0% | 0% |
| • Business Professional (analyst, buyer, consultant, accountant, planner, engineer, etc.) | 55% | 23% | 14% | 9% | 7% |
| • Manager | 11% | 53% | 35% | 17% | 13% |
| • Entrepreneur | 5% | 11% | 18% | 36% | 41% |
| • Executive | 2% | 12% | 31% | 36% | 39% |

11. Regarding their functional focus:

| | 1975 | 1979 | 1984 | 1989 |
|---|------|------|------|------|
| Marketing and Sales | 30% | 29% | 12% | 15% |
| Finance | 17% | 19% | 16% | 14% |
| Accounting/Control | 13% | 12% | 6% | 4% |
| General Management | 13% | 21% | 56% | 54% |
| Production/Operations | 10% | 9% | 7% | 5% |
| All Other | 17% | 10% | 3% | 8% |

12. From *Statistical Abstracts of US, 1992*, Page 462, Table 732.

13. From *Federal Reserve Bulletin*, January 1992, Page 3.

14. Figures for the Class of '49 are medians as reported in *Fortune*, May 1974.

15. Here I am referring to 2012 dollars, not constant 1992 dollars.

*Chapter 2. Unconventional Career Paths*

1. In the early 1800s, New England textile firms were among the largest businesses in the United States, yet they typically had only 75–80 employees. Also, see the discussion in *The Visible Hand* by Alfred Chandler Jr., Cambridge, Mass: Belnap Press of Harvard University, 1977. Chandler argues that before 1860, the vast majority of the working population were employed in organizations with fewer than 1,000 people. In the 1860s and '70s, technological developments associated with the Industrial Revolution created the conditions under which many medium-sized and large organizations began to emerge in the United States. Small businesses were not equipped to build regional and national railroad systems, so bigger firms were created to do the job. The same was true for the telegraph and telephone. As these communication and transportation systems created larger and larger markets for goods, bigger factories were built to take advantage of the economies of scale made possible by new technologies. As increasing numbers of goods and services were produced more cheaply, standards of living and life expectancies went up, which meant still bigger markets, the possibility of bigger factories and stores to serve those markets, and so on.

2. See Chandler.

3. See J. H. S. Bossard and J. F. Dewurt, *University Education for Business*, Philadelphia: University of Pennsylvania Press, 1931.

4. See *And Mark an Era* by Mclvin T. Copeland, Boston: Little Brown, 1958, Page 72.

5. See Bossard and Dewurt, op. cit., Page 23.

6. This work is described in detail in *Management and the Worker* by Fritz Roethlisberger and William Dickson, Cambridge, Mass.: Harvard University Press, 1938.

7. Regarding where Harvard MBAs, Class of '74, are working 1975–1991:*

|                                          | 1975  | 1983  | 1992  |
| ---------------------------------------- | ----- | ----- | ----- |
| Very Small (1–100 Employees)             | 7%    | 22%   | 33%   |
|                                          | >28%  | >43%  | >62%  |
| Small (101–1,000 Employees)              | 21%   | 21%   | 29%   |
| Medium (1,001–10,000 Employees)          | 35%   | 26%   | 15%   |
| Large (10,001–100,000 Employees)         | 33%   | 28%   | 20%   |
|                                          | >36%  | >31%  | >23%  |
| Very Large (100,001 + Employees)         | 3%    | 3%    | 3%    |

*Does not include people who have retired or dropped out of MBA-like careers (e.g., a writer).

8. Credible statistics are hard to find. For reasons explained in Chapter 5, significant numbers of Harvard MBAs have always gone into small businesses. But that percentage appears to have been increasing over the past three or four decades.

9. This figure is based on a questionnaire given to alumni from that class at their 30th reunion in 1989.

10. From Page 50 in *Social Structure and Learning Climate* by Charles Orth, Boston: Division of Research, Graduate School of Business Administration, Harvard University, 1963.

11. At the other extreme, a few would have correctly predicted that many graduates were going to be entrepreneurs. But this group of faculty was a clear minority.

12. Regarding income differentials between those who capitalized on post '73 opportunities and those who did not:

|                                | 1991 Median Total Income | 1991 Mean Total Income |
| ------------------------------ | ------------------------ | ---------------------- |
| Small Business                 | $200,000                 | $400,000               |
| Medium and Large Businesses    | $180,000                 | $267,000               |

|  | 1991 Median<br>Total Income | 1991 Mean<br>Total Income |
|---|---|---|
| Entrepreneurs | $210,000 | $612,000 |
| Non-entrepreneurs | $165,000 | $178,000 |
| Non-manufacturing | $200,000 | $390,000 |
| Manufacturing | $150,000 | $170,000 |

13. Regarding title differences between those who capitalized on post '73 opportunities and those who did not:

|  | % With Titles of Chairman,<br>President, CEO, or COO |
|---|---|
| Small Business | 42% |
| Medium and Large Business | 16% |
| Entrepreneur | 56% |
| Non-entrepreneur | 15% |
| Non-manufacturing | 33% |
| Manufacturing | 31% |

*Chapter 3. The Post '73 Economic Environment*

1. Michael Jensen has also recently concluded that 1973 marked the beginning of a new economic age. His argument is interesting because it is based on an analysis that, in some ways, is quite different from the one offered in this book. See "The Modern Industrial Revolution and the Challenge to Internal Control Systems," *Journal of Finance*, July 1993, Pages 831–881.

2. See *The Prize* by Daniel Yergin, New York: Simon & Schuster, 1992, Pages 605–615.

3. This way of thinking about big company capitalism in the United States has roots in the works of at least a dozen different people. However, the specific formulation presented here and summarized in Exhibit 3.1 was developed in conjunction with writing this book.

4. See Alfred Chandler, Jr., *The Visible Hand*, Cambridge: Harvard University Press, 1977.

5. Of the 495 important inventions, discoveries, and innovations listed in the *1993 World Almanac*, 145 are attributed to the United States during the period 1860 to 1930, with most of that concentrated in 1880 to 1930. No other fifty year period in any country at any time has a higher rate of discovery/invention/innovation. See Pages 178–181.

6. 1930 statistic from *1993 World Almanac*, Page 395. Earlier statistic is for Massachusetts in 1855. From *Historical Statistics: Colonial Times to 1970*, U.S. Bureau of the Census, Washington, D.C.: U.S. Government Printing Office, 1970, Page 56.

7. From *Historical Statistics: Colonial Times to 1970*, U.S. Bureau of the Census, Washington, D.C.: U.S. Government Printing Office, 1970, Page 56.

8. The 1970 figure is from *1993 World Almanac*, Page 395. The 1930 figure is an estimate based on 1990 official definitions of poverty, median family size in 1930, median family income in 1929, and CPI inflation convertors. The 1929 income figures are from Brookings Institute data reported in *Breaking Point* by Kevin Phillips, New York: Random House, 1993.

9. Statistics from *The Work of Nations* by Robert B. Reich, New York: Vintage, 1992, Page 56.

10. *Direction of Trade Statistics Yearbook*, International Monetary Fund, 1974–1992.

11. Figures are for unit production in 1974 and 1989. See *Industrial Statistics Yearbook*, United Nations, 1976 and 1989 Editions.

12. See *Annual Statistical Report*, American Iron and Steel Institute, 1976 and 1991 Editions.

13. For unit production in 1974 and 1989. See *Industrial Statistics Yearbook*, United Nations, 1976 and 1991 Editions.

14. See *Ward's Automotive Yearbook*, Ward's Communications, 1975 and 1991 Editions.

15. See *Corporate Culture and Performance*, by John P. Kotter and James L. Heskett, New York: Free Press, 1992.

16. From *1993 World Almanac*, Page 160.

17. See *The Work of Nations* by Robert B. Reich, New York: Vintage, 1992, Page 105.

18. See *Liar's Poker,* by Michael Lewis, New York: Norton, 1989, Pages 35, 36.

19. All numbers from Kemper Financial Services.

20. See *The Work of Nations,* New York: Knopf, 1991, Pages 82, 83.

21. See David L. Birch, "The Hidden Economy," in *The Wall Street Journal,* June 10, 1988, Page 23R.

22. The top 5% income earners in the United States received 34% of total individual income in 1928. By 1946, their share fell by nearly half, to 18%. During this same period, the top 1% of earners saw their incomes drop from 19% of the total to 7.7%. See *Historical Statistics of the United States: Colonial Times to 1957,* U.S. Bureau of the Census, Washington, D.C.: U.S. Government Printing Office, 1960. The share of aggregate gross income of the richest 0.5% of taxpayers continued to decline almost steadily even in the 1950s and 1960s before bottoming out in 1973 and then starting to go up again. See "Inequality and Its Charms" by Robert Barro, *Wall Street Journal,* February 10, 1993, Editorial Page.

23. From 1977 to 1990, income of the poorest fifth of Americans dropped about 5%. From *The Work of Nations,* by Robert B. Reich, New York: Vintage, 1992, Page 7. The gap in income between the top 1% of families and the next 19% also grew. See Page 279 in Kevin Phillips' *Boiling Point,* New York: Random House, 1993.

24. See, for example, *The Cost of Talent* by Derek Bok, New York: Free Press, 1993.

25. See, for example, "Reemployment Increases among Displaced Workers," U.S. Department of Labor, Bureau of Labor Statistics, *BLS News,* USDL 86-414, October 14, 1986.

26. As reported in *USA Today,* March 1, 1993, Page 7C. The NFL Players Association announced in September 1993 that average 1993 salaries were $643,000.

27. Statistics from various issues of *The American Lawyer.*

28. AMA and Census data.

29. See, for example, "Reconciling Conflicting Data on Jobs for College Graduates" by Daniel Hecker in *Monthly Labor Review*, July 1992.

30. See Page 355 in *The World Almanac 1994*.

31. As reported in *Financial World* magazine.

32. As reported in "Inequality and Its Charms" by Robert Barro, *Wall Street Journal*, February 10, 1993, Editorial Page.

33. See Page 143, *Annual Energy Review*, 1988.

34. Statistics from the Federal Reserve.

35. Also see Reich's discussion in *The Work of Nations*, New York: Vintage, 1992, Page 202.

*Chapter 4. Founding and Growing Small Businesses*

1. Because small firms are much less likely than large ones to offer summer jobs to young people, collegians who want to work in small businesses often end up working in large enterprises during summer months.

2. This relationship can be seen even within the class:

| | Working in Manufacturing | Working in Non-manufacturing |
|---|---|---|
| Large Firms | 40% | 60% |
| Medium Firms | 24% | 76% |
| Small Firms | 17% | 83% |

3. From "The Fortune Director, 1958," a supplement to the August 1958 *Fortune* magazine.

4. *Fortune*, July 27, 1992, Guide to the Global 500.

5. From the *Economist*, February 3, 1986.

6. *Fortune*, August 24, 1992, Pages 213, 214.

7. Many people have documented this including myself. See, for example, three of my books: *The Leadership Factor*, Free Press, 1988, *A Force for Change: How Leadership Differs from Management*, Free Press, 1990, and *Corporate Culture and Performance*, with Jim Heskett, Free Press, 1992.

8. See, for example, *Prophets in the Dark* by David Kearns and David Nadler, New York: Harper Business, 1992.

9. *Newsweek* had done a cover story called "The Blue-Collar Blues" in 1971 (May 17 edition, story on Pages 80–86).

10. See Chapter 4 in *Work Redesign* by Richard Hackman and Greg Oldham, Reading, Mass.: Addison-Wesley, 1980.

11. Regarding satisfaction possibilities in firms of different sizes:

|  | Small | Medium | Large |
|---|---|---|---|
| • Job allows autonomy | 6.36 | 5.95 | 5.74 |
| • Job is whole piece of work | 6.02 | 5.53 | 5.29 |
| • Job itself gives information on work performance | 5.79 | 5.03 | 5.38 |

Scale = 1 - 7 e.g., *1* = *very little*—the job gives me almost no personal "say" about how and when the work is done. *4* = *moderate autonomy*— many things were standardized and not under my control, but I can make some decisions about the work; *7* = *very much*— . . . complete responsibility. From Appendix A, *Work Redesign* by Richard Hackman and Greg Oldham, Reading, Mass.: Addison-Wesley, 1980.

12. See *In Search of Excellence*, New York: Harper and Row, 1982.

13. On the surface, Exhibits 4.4 and 2.4 may seem inconsistent. They are not. Income differences are larger in 2.4 because a) the figures reported are means not medians and b) the figures include differences for entrepreneurs versus non-entrepreneurs and non-manufacturing versus manufacturing.

14. Source: Kemper Financial Services.

15. Source: A study by American Express, reported in *Fortune*, June 14, 1993, Page 10.

16. As reported in *Fortune*, June 14, 1993, Page 22.


*Chapter 5. Consulting to and Assisting Big Business*

1. See *The Age of Unreason*, Boston: Harvard Business School Press, 1990.

2. See, for example, *Networks and Organizations: Structure, Form and Action*, edited by Nitin Nohria and Robert G. Eccles, Boston, Mass.: HBS Press, 1992.

3. See Mike Hammer and Jim Champy, *Re-engineering the Corporation*, New York: HarperBusiness, 1993.

4. I have discussed this point in much more detail in my 1985 book *Power and Influence: Beyond Formal Authority*, New York: Free Press.

5. For a discussion of the company boundaries point, see Joseph L. Badaracco, Jr., *The Knowledge Link*, Boston: HBS Press, 1991.

6. The evidence supporting this broad generalization can be found in many reports over the last decade. See, for example, two of my books: *The General Managers* (New York: Free Press, 1982) and *Power and Influence: Beyond Formal Authority* (New York: The Free Press, 1985).

7. Placement statistics are based on questionnaires given to graduating MBAs by the HBS Office of Career Development.

8. From questionnaires filled out by about 20% of the overall class. Source: HBS Placement Office.

9. Source: *Consultants News*, September, 1992, Kennedy Publications, Fitzwilliam, NH, Page 1.

10. See "Workers Are Forced to Take More Jobs with Few Benefits," by Clare Ansberry, *Wall Street Journal*, March 11, 1993, Page 1.

11. See the *Business Week* cover story from the April 12, 1993 edition, Pages 58–65.

*Chapter 6. Providing Leadership*

1. This work is described in more detail in my book *A Force for Change: How Leadership Differs from Management*, New York: Free Press, 1990.

2. These findings about leadership are consistent with other major leadership studies reported recently. See, for example, *Leaders* by Warren Bennis and Burt Nanis, New York: Harper, 1985.

3. In addition to the evidence presented in *A Force For Change*, see also *Corporate Culture and Performance*, my 1992 book (with Jim Heskett), New York: Free Press.

4. For a good example of this kind of change, and the leadership that drives it, see *Control Your Destiny or Someone Else Will* by Noel Tichy and Stratford Sherman, New York: Doubleday, 1993.

5. See the evidence in *Corporate Culture and Performance*, especially Chapter 4.

6. See my *Corporate Culture and Performance* book.

7. I have found this on-the-job development process in a number of studies. See, for example, Chapter 3 in *The General Managers*, New York: Free Press, 1982.

8. In a series of studies done in 1985, 1986, and 1987, I found that large companies often had cultures that systematically undermined their ability to develop sufficient leadership capability in their executive ranks. See *The Leadership Factor*, New York: Free Press, 1988.

9. For a further discussion of this, see Chapter 8 in *A Force for Change*, New York: Free Press, 1990.

10. When the required Business Policy course was taught by certain senior faculty, it probably was a relatively strong course in leadership. But that was not the normal case.

*Chapter 7. Doing Deals*

1. Statistics from *The Death of Organization Man* by Amanda Bennett, New York: William Morrow, 1990, Page 131.

2. See *The Wealth of Nations*, 1776.

3. Source: the analysis of a variety of psychological test data collected from one half of the total group in 1973.

4. See Page 24 in *Liar's Poker* by Michael Lewis, New York: Norton, 1989.

*Chapter 8. Competitive Drive*

1. Regarding gender, race, nationality, and social class:

| Parents' Socioeconomic Status | White U.S. Men | All Other U.S. Men | Foreign Men | All Women |
|---|---|---|---|---|
| Upper Class | 10 (9%) | 0% | 4(4%) | 2(2%) |
| Upper Middle Class | 42(37%) | 1(1%) | 9(8%) | 4(4%) |
| Middle Class | 23(20%) | 0% | 1(1%) | 1(1%) |
| Lower Middle Class | 12(11%) | 1(1%) | 1(1%) | 0% |
| Lower Class | 0% | 1(1%) | 0% | 0% |

Source: Self-report.

2. Regarding family income in 1960:

| | Family of '74 MBAs | All U.S. Families* |
|---|---|---|
| $0–2999 | 4% | 21% |
| $3000–5999 | 11% | 33% |
| $6000–11,999 | 38% | 35% |
| $12,000–29,999 | 28% | 8% |
| $30,000–149,000 | 17% | 1% |

*Data compiled from *Census of Population*, 1960: Final Report PC (2)-4b. Washington, D.C.

3. Regarding father's and mother's educational level:

| | Fathers of of '74 MBAs | Fathers of All Graduate Students (mid-'60s)* | All U.S. Men (1972–82)[†] | Mothers of '74 MBAs | Mothers of All Graduate Students (mid-'60s) | All U.S. Women (1972–82)[†] |
|---|---|---|---|---|---|---|
| Grade School or less | 5% | 13% | 36% | 4% | 9% | 34% |
| Some High School | 9% | 28% | 9% | 5% | 27% | 12% |
| High School Grad | 10% | 23% | 16% | 28% | 34% | 24% |
| Some College | 20% | 12% | 9% | 24% | 16% | 6% |
| College Grad | 28% | 12% | 4% | 28% | 11% | 4% |
| Master's Degree | 18% | 4% | 2% | 12% | 1% | 1% |
| Ph.D. or equivalent | 10% | 8% | 1% | 0% | 1% | 0% |

*Data compiled from *Digest of Educational Statistics*, U.S. Department of Education, Washington, D.C., 1969.
[†]Data compiled from *General Social Surveys* (1972–1982), National Opinion Research Center; University of Chicago, 1972–1982.

4. Regarding father's occupation:

|  | '74 MBAs | All Graduate Students (mid-60s)* | All Male U.S. Workers 1960[†] |
|---|---|---|---|
| Managers | 35% | 18% | 11% |
| Professionals | 31% | 24% | 11% |
| White Collar | 14% | 38% | 20% |
| Blue Collar | 16% | 19% | 48% |

*Data compiled from *Digest of Educational Statistics*, U.S. Department of Education, Washington, D.C., 1969.
[†]Data compiled from *Census of Population*, 1960. Final Report PC (2)-7a. Washington, D.C.

5. Regarding net worth of parents and grandparents at age 60 in 1984 dollars:

|  | Parents | Paternal Grandparents | Maternal Grandparents |
|---|---|---|---|
| $0–4999 | 2% | 9% | 11% |
| $5,000–19,999 | 7% | 21% | 24% |
| $20,000–99,999 | 23% | 36% | 29% |
| $100,000–499,999 | 36% | 19% | 18% |
| $500,000–2.5 mil | 25% | 12% | 11% |
| $more than 2.5 mil | 9% | 4% | 7% |
| Median | $200,000 | $60,000 | $60,000 |

6. Regarding quality of their colleges:

| | |
|---|---|
| Most Competitive and Highly Competitive | 55% |
| Very Competitive and Competitive | 42% |
| Less Competitive | 1% |
| Non-competitive | 2% |

Source: Data adapted from *Barron's Profiles of American Colleges*, Woodbury, N.Y.: Barron's Educational Series, 1980. The vast majority of schools in the United States are rated "less competitive" and "non-competitive." Non-U.S. schools are omitted from the Exhibit.

7. Regarding college academic performance:

| | |
|---|---|
| Top 1% | 9% |
| Top 5% | 31% |
| Top 10% | 52% |
| Top 25% | 77% |

Source: Self-report.

8. Regarding percentage of MBAs participating in extracurricular activities in college and high school:

| | | | |
|---|---|---|---|
| Member of social academic club | 87% | One of top five officers in social/academic club | 55% |
| Member of student government | 68% | One of top five officers in student government | 34% |
| Member of varsity team | 60% | Captain or co-captain of a varsity team | 26% |
| On the staff of a publication | 45% | One of top five officers on a publication board | 29% |
| Member of a musical or dramatic group | 40% | One of top five officers in a musical/dramatic group | 9% |

Source: Self-report.

9. Regarding undergraduate major:

| | '74 MBAs | All U.S. (in 1967–68)* |
|---|---|---|
| Engineering | 32% | 6% |
| Economics | 18% | 2% |
| Other social sciences | 15% | 17% |
| Business administration | 10% | 13% |
| Physical sciences, biological sciences, and math | 11% | 12% |
| Humanities | 11% | 16% |

*Source: *Digest of Educational Statistics,* U.S. Department of Education; Washington, D.C., 1969, Page 82, Table 112.

10. Regarding GMAT scores:

|  | Class of '74 | All Test Takers in 1972* |
|---|---|---|
| Top 25% Median | 649 | 525 |
| Overall Median Score | 625 | 475 |
| Bottom 25% Median | 587 | 400 |

*Source: Data complied from *Guide to Use of ATGSB Scores—72–73*, ETS; Princeton, N.J., 1973.

11. Regarding values*:

|  | Class of '74 | 8369 College Students[†] | 5894 College Males[†] |
|---|---|---|---|
| Theoretical | 41.47 | 39.80 | 43.09 |
| Economic | 45.61 | 39.45 | 42.05 |
| Aesthetic | 41.73 | 40.29 | 36.22 |
| Social | 38.44 | 39.34 | 37.05 |
| Political | 46.46 | 40.61 | 43.22 |
| Religious | 25.92 | 40.51 | 37.88 |

*Mean scores from Allport, Vernon, Lindzey "Study of Values" questionnaire.
[†]Data adapted from "Study of Values, Manual," from Allport, Vernon, and Lindzey, Boston: Houghton Mifflin, 1960, Page 11.

Regarding common themes found in psychological test data and personal histories:

| Theme | % with Theme | Theme | % with Theme |
|---|---|---|---|
| Power-Status | 84% | Nonwork Relations | 61% |
| Group Worker | 65% | Money-Security | 57% |
| Pragmatic | 62% | Independent | 54% |
| Variety | 62% | | |

12. Half of the group took an elective course in the fall of 1973 called "Self Assessment and Career Development." Through the use of psychological tests and other written exercises, students were encouraged to become more aware of what their aspirations were. My conclusions about the dreams they shared is based on the information generated in that course.

13. Regarding their evaluation of educational experiences:

|                | Pre-College | College | HBS  |
|----------------|-------------|---------|------|
| Was enjoyable  | 3.83        | 3.84    | 3.57 |
| Was difficult  | 2.83        | 3.29    | 3.60 |
| Was worthwhile | 3.79        | 4.01    | 4.30 |

Scale: 1 = Never, 2 = Rarely, 3 = Sometimes, 4 = Often, 5 = Almost Always.

14. These conclusions about the impact of the program are based first on answers supplied by the Class of '74 and second on my own personal experiences at Harvard over the past 20 years.

15. I use "signal" here in the sense that the word has been developed by Mike Spence. See "Job Market Signaling," *Quarterly Journal of Economics*, 87, August 1973, Pages 355–374.

16. In 1973, 59 of the 115 participants took a series of psychological tests as a part of a course entitled "Self Assessment and Career Development." These tests were then used to identify major themes for each individual. Because this work was done in 1973, it is not possible that the results were biased by our knowledge of subsequent economic results.

17. Parental socioeconomic class is a powerful force in shaping lives. Dozens of studies have shown this to be true. For example, Blau and Duncan report a .40 correlation between father's occupation and son's occupation. See P. M. Blau and O. D. Duncan, *The American Occupational Structure*, New York: Wiley, 1967. The higher the social status of Class of '74 parents, the more one tends to find non-working mothers, fathers who were oriented to work and career, both parents happy with dad's career progress, better-educated neighbors, a close relationship with dad, mothers who did not pressure the children to do well, fathers who were admired and were seen as role models, higher economic expectations on the part of the children, more children in prep school, more children attending a high-status college, and fewer children saying that college was lonely. At least two of the three measures of parental social class correlate with all these factors (statistically significant at .05 or better). But despite all the evidence that parental social class is very important, statistics do not show that it is a major driving force in determing Class of '74 income. If it were, children of upper-middle-class families

would on average be making money like these 115 individuals, and that is far from the case. Also, if family economic background was important in this way, those in the class from poorer families would on average be making much less today than those from rich families, but they are not. Within the Class of '74, there is virtually no relationship between background affluence and 1991 income.

| Parental Net Worth at Age 60 (in 1984 Dollars) | Median 1991 MBA Income |
|---|---|
| $500,000 or more | $180,000 |
| $100,000–$499,999 | $190,000 |
| 0–$99,000 | $185,000 |

18. Like parental socioeconomic class, measures of intelligence have been shown to be important in shaping careers. Some occupations appear to demand more intellectual capacity than others, both in the work itself and in the schooling required to obtain that work. Nevertheless, *within* the Class of '74, there is virtually no relationship between measures of intelligence and income.

19. For now, those unwilling or unable to compete are going to find life at work increasingly unpleasant, regardless of who holds power in Washington. The most relevant unit of analysis today is no longer the nation; it is the entire earth. In an increasingly interdependent world economy, presidents of countries no longer have the power to do what Roosevelt and others did sixty years ago. For example, sixty years ago, it was difficult for individuals or companies to move from high-tax/high-regulation areas to lower-tax /lower-regulation areas. Increasingly, this is becoming easier. Reich says: "Throughout the 1980s, the . . . high technology zone encircling Boston shifted outward to southern New Hampshire and northern Rhode Island, as symbolic analysts chose to live and work where taxes were lower. Researchers have documented a similar movement by skilled immigrants from nations where they are compelled to share a larger portion of their incomes to nations that tax them less. The 'brain drain' from egalitarian Europe to less egalitarian America offers some evidence of this phenomenon. Another illustration is found in immigration patterns between the United States and Canada. Most of the

Americans who immigrate to Canada have been relatively low-skilled routine producers or in-person servers; most of the Canadians who have come to the United States have been high-skilled symbolic analysts. Why? Both nations offer a similar array of job possibilities. But a pertinent difference is that Canada has more egalitarian distribution of income and offers more generous social services than does the United States. Thus do un-skilled Americans find in Canada a hospitable environment where they can enjoy greater income security; and thus do skilled Canadians find in the United States a hospitable environment where they can retain more of their earnings for themselves." From *The Work of Nations* by Robert B. Reich, New York: Vintage, 1992, Page 299. A 1990s repeat of the 1930s would require a powerful and enlightened United Nations or a wise President of Earth. Neither yet exists.

### Chapter 9. Lifelong Learning

1. Those who study careers have been remarking on this change for at least a decade. See, for example, Rosabeth Kanter's discussion of this in *When Giants Learn to Dance: Mastering the Challenge of Strategy, Management, and Careers in the 1990s*, New York: Simon and Schuster, 1989.

2. This pattern of turning difficult experiences into growth has been well documented in the case of successful executives by Morgan McCall, Mike Lombardo, and Ann Morrison. See their book *The Lessons of Experience*, Lexington, Mass.: Lexington Books, 1988, especially Chapter 4.

### Chapter 10. Success at Work

1. Initially, most were exceptionally career focused. When asked to rank a list of thirty-two items in terms of how important each issue was in their lives immediately after graduation, they placed "achieving recognition on the job" first, "learning the skills needed for job mastery" second, and "gaining respect from your boss" third. The six lowest-rated items were: "finding a spouse," "resolving a difficult issue with your spouse," "spiritual or religious development," "becoming integrated in

community activities," "switching employers," and "having a child."

2. I have looked for other age related patterns and have found very few. Even the famous "midlife crisis" does not seem to be that universal or influential in this group. Longitudinal data on how they feel about aspects of life do not vary much or fall into obvious patterns. At one point, when I began to wonder if I was overlooking something, I found the following graph in a new book by David Myers:

### Age and Well-Being In Sixteen Nations

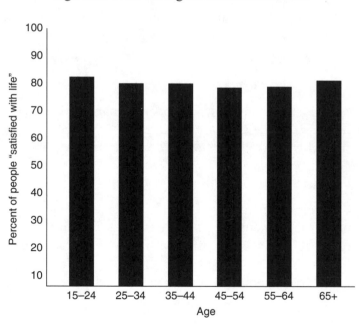

Source: Data from 169,776 people as reported by Ronald Inglehart in *Culture Shift in Advanced Industrial Society*, Princeton: Princeton University Press, 1990.

3. See Chapter 5 in *The Cost of Talent* by Derek Bok, New York: Free Press, 1993.

4. See Graef S. Crystal's excellent work on this—*In Search of Excess*, New York: Norton, 1992.

5. The stories of useful change in government found in David Osborne's and Ted Gaebler's *Reinventing Government* (Reading, Mass.: Addison Wesley, 1992) are almost all examples of movement from tall hierarchies toward flexible networks.

6. Source: *World Almanac* 1994, Page 358.

*Chapter 11. Education for the 21st Century*

1. The labor force and wage data presented here come from my colleague, Mike Jensen. See Table I in his "The Modern Industrial Revolution and the Challenge to Internal Control Systems," *Journal of Finance*, July 1993, Pages 831–881.

2. See, for example, the prescriptions in Lester Thurow's *Head to Head*, New York: William Morrow, 1992.

3. Page 286 in *Head to Head*, New York: Warner Books, 1992.

4. See Census Bureau data.

5. See Education 1990, *Fortune*, Special Issue, Page 54.

6. From Secretary of Labor Robert B. Reich, *The Work of Nations*, New York: Vintage Books, 1992, Page 227.

7. See *Science Achievement in 17 Countries: A Preliminary Report* by the International Association for the Evaluation of Educational Achievement, New York: Pergamon Press, 1988, and "Foreigners Outpace American Students in Science" by Robert Rothman, *Education Week*, January 28, 1987, Page 1.

8. See *Thinking for a Living*, New York: Basic Books, 1992, Page 80.

9. The first of these to receive widespread attention was *A Nation at Risk: The Imperative for Educational Reform* by the National Commission on Excellence in Education, Washington, D.C.: U.S. Government Printing Office, 1983.

10. An initiative like "Goals for the Year 2000" set by governors and former President Bush could make a difference, but as of this writing it is too early to tell what impact it will have.

11. Data on elementary and secondary education from the *Digest of Educational Statistics 1993*.

12. New York: Basic Books, 1992, Page 110.

13. This entire discussion about unadaptive cultures draws heavily from *Corporate Culture and Performance* by John Kotter and James Heskett, New York: Free Press, 1992.

14. Not everyone agrees with this assessment. For an interesting dissenting view, see Myron Lieberman's *Public Education: An Autopsy*, Cambridge, Mass.: Harvard University Press, 1993.

15. *Digest of Educational Statistics 1992*, Table 31, Page 34, and *United States Office of Education—Biannual Survey*, 1944–46, Page 38, Table XX.

16. See, for example, Lyman Porter and Lawrence McKibbin, *Management Education and Development*, New York: McGraw-Hill, 1988.

17. *Digest of Education Statistics*, 1992, Pages 285, 286.

18. *The Wall Street Journal*, January 21, 1993, Page 1.

# INDEX

# ABOUT THE AUTHOR

JOHN P. KOTTER is Konosuke Matsushita Professor of Leadership at the Harvard Business School and an internationally recognized authority on managerial behavior and leadership. Professor Kotter is a winner of the prestigious McKinsey Award for his articles in the *Harvard Business Review* and has received the Johnson Smith & Knisely Award for new perspectives on executive leadership. He lives in Cambridge, Massachusetts, with wife Nancy Dearman, daughter Caroline, and son Jonathan.